WHERE ARE WE?

WHERE ARE WE?

Thoughts from an American Geezer

RUDIE TRETTEN

ISBN: 10: 146366107X

ISBN 13: 978-1463661076

Library of Congress Control Number: 2011911175
CreateSpace, North Charleston, SC

DEDICATION

*These essays are dedicated to all the geezers around us
and to anyone who enjoys a spirited discussion about life.*

ACKNOWLEDGMENTS

This book would not have been published without the advice and editing of Peter and Paulette Zachariou, who are truly good, honest, and skilled professionals.

I would also like to express my appreciation to Paulette Sylvester for her great help in word processing all my handwritten drafts.

The staff at CreateSpace was also helpful, especially Gaines Hill.

Last but certainly not least, I thank my wife, Shirley, who dared to correct my work — and, in this process, made me a better writer.

ABOUT THE AUTHOR

Rudie Tretten was born in 1931 in Los Angeles, California. When he was eight, his family moved to San Francisco, where he attended public schools.

For almost all of his adult life, he has been involved in education. He earned a B.A. in political science from the University of California–Berkeley, an M.A in English from San Francisco State University, and a Ph.D. in social science education from Stanford University.

He has served in education in many roles: teacher, counselor, administrator, college instructor, college program director, supervisor, and consultant. As an instructor, he was known for using dialogue and humor and for playing devil's advocate to challenge his students to develop their thinking. He also served as a school board member for many years in the Pacifica School District in Pacifica, California.

During these years, he contributed to writing social science textbooks, curriculum for educational leadership, and research on project-based learning.

Between 2007 and 2011 he has written over three hundred short essays on such topics as education, politics, society, economics, aging, sports, incidental life experiences, and personal life. In some of these, he reflects on history, both social and personal, but in most, he presents his current thinking, questions, opinions, and feelings on current matters.

Since 1966 he has lived in Pacifica with Shirley, his wife of fifty-seven years. They have two adult children, one a nurse and the other a school principal.

CONTENTS

INTRODUCTION

The writer of these essays is, in fact, a geezer: "an eccentric, elderly man" of some eighty years. As youngsters, we were always *"going on…"* (e.g., not aged nine, but *going on* ten) in our urge to be older. I still want to get older, but now for a fundamentally different reason.

The subject matter of this book represents a spectrum of my interests and experiences over the years. My observations come from the time period of 2007–2011. I make reference to my *geezerness* in some essays, but they are all written from that perspective.

I am a "New Deal Democrat." I believe government can play a role in making society more equitable and in assisting its citizens who are in need. For this to happen, a means for countervailing power is required within the political/economic system to limit the potential of the most powerful. In an ideal world, this would not be necessary, but we are all subject to temptation. If we have learned anything from the recent financial crisis and recession, it is that unregulated markets, and participants in those markets, are subject to greed and the lust for power, with little thought for society as a whole.

I grew up in a Republican family. My mother voted for one Democratic presidential candidate, FDR, in his first run. My uncle, an M.D., was firm in his belief that President Roosevelt suffered not from polio but from syphilis.

My father was conservative, too, but he loved to take the opposite side in political arguments and generate fervent discussions.

From this background, I went to the University of California in February, 1949. A proof of my *geezerness* is the motto of my graduating class, created by my fraternity brother Jim Smith: *"Oskie wow wow, whiskey wee, we're the class of '53."*

My father died in 1977. I marveled at the changes he had lived through in his life. It's a big jump from the horse and buggy to man walking on the moon. But looking back at my life, I am astonished at the distance between the big radio in the living room of my childhood and the Internet world we live in now.

So we geezers have a perspective on our world today. However, like eyewitnesses to a crime, our perceptions and understanding of what we have lived through vary.

My personal responses to life from 1931 to 2011 are not meant to be a unified geezer view of the world. That does not exist.

I chose the five major topic areas for my essays because they are of interest to me, and I have some background in each. The essays also represent ideas, issues, and experiences that have activated my mind and my pen.

For instance, the political process is critical to the functioning of a democracy. Since democracy is our goal as a nation, we must pay attention to the manner in which we pursue that goal. Our politics function within a socioeconomic system that is under intense pressure. Our political response to these pressures will be a measure of our willingness to confront reality rather than surrender to ideology.

For example, under the heading "Politics," I have written about individual responsibilities, power, the political process, and so forth.

I also composed some pieces dealing with economics and the recent ongoing recession, the importance of regulation, changes in our economy, and related ideas.

Because of our economic problems, our education system from prekindergarten through graduate school is going through cutbacks. Do we believe that public education is a principal component within a democratic society? My essays also look at education today and comment upon the difficulties encountered by school administrators, the role of expectations in educational success, and the ascendancy of female students in our schools and colleges.

I enjoy sports. I am not an athlete and have not found great success in the games I have played. On several occasions, I have been a sports writer. I comment on athletics as a superannuated tennis player and a baseball fan. Life has a lighter side, even though sports often reflect serious social concerns.

It has been fun for me to write these essays. I even enjoy re-reading them! I hope they trigger some thoughts and feelings from my fellow geezers and others approaching this exalted station in life.

SOCIETY

Society has become much more complex in the past eighty years. Civil rights successes, changing demographics, new laws, technology, and dramatically changed international power structures all contribute to the confusion this oldster often feels. I've lived through it all and have perspectives on these changes; therefore, I write about them.

ADJUSTING

"Yes, you're right, the carburetor does need adjustment. Leave the car here, and I'll have it for you tomorrow." A quick diagnosis of the problem and an overnight solution. Simply an adjustment. Just like the good ole USA in 2009, except that we have more than one adjustment to make. Maybe ten.

To *undaunt* our task, we'll cut the number to five. The chosen exemplars of our current and future lifestyle arrangements are:

1) Recreating our economy;
2) (Related to #1) Moving from carbon-based power to a multiplicity of power sources for the economy;
3) (Related to #1 & #2) Recognizing that there are limits to how much we, as a society, can consume;
4) Developing a new approach to foreign policy that acknowledges the new multipolar world that confronts us and the declining value of our current military;
5) (A part of #1 with #4) Responding to the changing economic, political, and social role of women in the United States and the world.

To personalize this, I ask myself, "How do I, a seventy-eight-year-old white male, adjust to a world that will soon be upside down relative to the world I grew up in?" OK, so I won't be around long enough to have to do a lot of adjusting. But working down the age groupings to those who are in their twenties, it is clear that much of our population will be involved in an enormous process of lifestyle changes.

Number five on our abbreviated catalogue of adjustments can serve as the starting point for our squint at our future carburetor. While I have written in the past about the ascent of women in American society, two recent articles in respected journals clearly delineate what is occurring worldwide regarding the rise of female power. Reihan Salam, in an issue of *Foreign Policy*, and Katty Kay and Claire Shipman, in the *Washington Post*, laid out the case for the rise of women and the concurrent decline of the testosterone-laden sex.

For example, 80 percent of job losses in the United States during the recession have been among men. Some commentators have renamed our economic woes a "he-cession." Job losses have taken place disproportionately in economic sectors traditionally dominated by men, such as construction and manufacturing. This has occurred while job fields identified as women's work — teaching, nursing, social service — have been more secure. In his *Foreign Policy* article, Salam observes that these trends are present in Europe as well. He writes that by the end of 2009, twenty-eight million men will be jobless throughout the world. Looking to the future and an economy based on knowledge-related skills, women are positioned to move into the new occupations emerging. Female college graduates in the United States will soon outnumber males three to two.

A similar trend is taking place throughout the developed world. Energy and the search for new sources of power will be major elements in the new economy. While science and engineering were recently bastions of male authority, women are now progressing in these fields.

As our new economy unfolds, women will be more than educated, knowledgeable entry-level employees. Kay and Shipman quote numerous studies showing the effectiveness of women in senior managerial positions — and how, with more women, the performance of companies increases.

Also, American families are saving more of their income these days. Here again, women are playing a major role. As the principal spenders in our families, their decisions are critical. How women respond to the new frugality will affect our economy and the global economy.

In terms of foreign policy, it may be significant that three of the last four secretaries of state have been women. The call for greater use of diplomacy and "soft power" — instead of the almost unconstrained reliance on military force — may reflect a more feminine, or less macho, approach to the world.

Some have equated the Wall Street excesses that have contributed to the recession with testosterone-fed overconfidence and risk taking, much like what took place in our adventure in Iraq.

So there you have it, youngsters. The future, if it is to be one of prosperity and peace, will be one in which women exercise more power and authority. Consequently, men will have to learn to work cooperatively and respectfully with women. What will happen to those who cannot manage this transition remains a major question.

Perhaps a recent incident involving my son and his wife illustrates the point. On vacation in Santa Barbara, they went to shoot a round of golf at one of the local courses. They were paired with two middle-aged men who happened to be managers in large corporations. Both were good enough at the game to have played in professional and amateur tournaments. On the third hole, my daughter-in-law hit a drive that went well beyond those of the men. She was congratulated on her accomplishment, but the sense was that this was an oddity and a bit of luck.

She refuted this by doing the same thing consistently through fifteen holes. Before the sixteenth, the two managerial types figured out that they had someplace else they had to be and left.

So what, if anything, are we to make of their adjustment to a new reality? Assuming the two golfers wanted to end their torment, walking away was an easy out. I hope that such avoidance will not be how we Americans respond to these changes.

ALL DAY WE FACE THE BARREN WASTE

Now we have yet another reason to pay attention to the evening news. There are still the economy, Afghanistan, Iraq, and other potential catastrophes. Add to the list: the weather. We're looking for rain in the forecast, but what we seem to be in store for is a third year of drought.

As I scribble these lines, I look out at our back patio where a half dozen or so azaleas are in bright bloom. White, pink, red, and scarlet. Their February blossoms are related to the sunny, warm weather we have enjoyed much of this winter.

Throughout our two dry years, I have kept this garden wet and fed the plants periodically. The resultant colors have been a joy to behold. The roses, too, have grown well, producing lovely flowers in a variety of colors. Now, in Drought Year Three, we hear about water rationing in our future.

Rationing is already a fact of life in some parts of the San Francisco Bay Area. The Sierra snowpack is down to about 60 percent of normal; the population is continuing to grow; and farmers are appealing for more water for their crops. Demand is up, and supply is down.

We are not alone as we cope with Jupiter Pluvius's failure to meet our needs. Australia is in its tenth year of drought. The problem is of such long standing that Australia now considers drought to be the normal condition. A big rainy season would be welcome, but the rain would be the exception for planning purposes.

One outcome of the Aussies coming to grips with their dry-ness has been the demise of the front lawn. Sports requiring large spaces of greensward, such as soccer or rugby, are under pressure.

As usual, in the creative California zeitgeist, there is a multitude of ideas for living with drought. One big-scale concept is transforming ocean water via desalinization. This has been done in the Middle East and in Santa Barbara. One big difficulty — it takes a lot of energy, and the energy problem is yet another dilemma facing the government.

We can use gray water from our showers and baths to soak our gardens. We can expand our efforts to purify our wastewater (this is being done on some golf courses). Restaurants could stop providing every customer with a glass of water and serve it only upon request.

There are still other water-saving strategies that can be implemented. Nations and regions all over the earth will be testing a variety of approaches.

Poverty-stricken Afghan villages enduring their own drought will now have something in common with affluent California.

Changing of the Guard?

What do I do when my grandson comes to visit and sees the cover of *Atlantic* that reads, in large letters, "The End of Men — How Women Are Taking Control of Everything"?

He's a high school junior with a driver's license and access to a pickup. He does well in school and has been chosen to participate in several special projects. In a couple more years, he'll be a man, a certified loser in the eyes of writer Hanna Rosin.

She describes how our changing economy is taking away jobs traditionally held by men, mainly in manufacturing, where strong unions kept salaries high enough to provide a middle-class life. With the stagnation of income in the 1970s and more women, particularly housewives, entering the job market, the male breadwinner's role began to diminish.

With emphasis on the service sector of the economy, where women have done relatively well in the past, young males now find themselves at an increasing disadvantage.

A college education is a necessity for these careers, and women now outnumber males as undergraduates, as well as in law and medical schools.

At some colleges, affirmative action programs are trying to increase male enrollment. There have always been enrollment programs favoring progeny of alumni and applicants with valued competencies, such as athletics and music. Affirmative action for men! Lordy, how that idea must shake the old white guys who are still resisting the idea of affirmative action for women and minorities.

In a way, this becomes a kind of payback for the years when women in college were channeled to education and nursing for careers. I know of cases when high school counselors advised excellent female math students to avoid thinking about mathematics, engineering, or the hard sciences as possible career choices. Women are still underrepresented in these professions.

Historically, boys in the early school years have not learned to read and write as quickly or as well as girls, and this hampered their progress in K–12 education. In the past, males attended college in greater numbers than did women — and the notion of a woman CEO was, "Well, maybe someday in the future." Now, Carly Fiorina and Meg Whitman, former CEOs of major corporations, are running for high political offices.

What to do now with the horde of potentially under- or unemployed men? Will they be able to acquire the unique attributes that Rosin identifies as female strengths in communication skills and social intelligence? More young bucks will have to attend college to gain the various certifications required for the available service sector jobs.

More attention is being devoted to attempts to promote greater male achievement in elementary schools so that they can do well in high school and, thus, make college a real possibility. *The American Prospect* magazine ran several articles on this topic in the same month as Rosin's *Atlantic* article appeared.

The current recession has shown that househusband is a viable male role, at least in the short run; but it does not correspond to the increasingly mythological "man of the family" role model.

We are, in so many ways, living in the middle of a continuous hurricane of change that requires adaptability and suspension of previously held shibboleths. Every day, the "truth" is being altered by events and new technologies. How much of the inevitable instability can we stand?

So, in answer to my puzzlement about my grandson seeing the "End of Men" cover, I think I'll put the magazine on the bottom of the pile. He's got enough to worry about.

❖ ❖ ❖

Contexts — Large and Small

"They took that quote out of context. If you read the sentence before the quoted segment and the sentence after it, you can understand what he really said."

Probably true, but the full five-page article establishes a broader context and provides added meaning through the details and examples cited.

Context is important in our daily lives. It is difficult to become engaged in a meaningful activity or conversation with another person if you don't share a similar context with your partner.

For example, if I go out with someone and buy a vanilla milkshake, he or she will no doubt assume that I really like vanilla. True, but there's a broader context, and it came to be on a recent trip to Hawaii.

My wife had seen an advertisement promoting a visit to a vanilla farm on the island of Hawaii. So off we went with directions in hand. After almost seventy miles, mostly on the main highway going from the Kona Coast to Hilo, we turned off onto a side road heading up the side of a hill. The road wound and turned through the tropical vegetation, and then we pulled into the parking area. We got out, ready to learn about vanilla farming.

We first encountered some people in a room that looked like a cafeteria. Two people, a man and a woman, were behind the counter separating the eating and food-preparation sections. We ordered. I had a strawberry milkshake made with vanilla ice cream. It was good. In fact, it was very good and eased both my thirst and hunger.

Another man entered the room. He was the owner of the farm — the only vanilla farm in the United States. Vanilla, it turns out, can only be grown in places twenty-five degrees or less from the equator, on hilly terrain, where there is plenty of water. Some seventy countries in the world grow vanilla. Madagascar and Indonesia are two of the largest producers.

So there was all this stuff to know about vanilla, but the real story was the farm family. Husband, wife, and five kids — three boys and two girls — ages four to fifteen.

They were being homeschooled, and each one had to contribute labor to the farm venture. The youngest worked an hour a day. After age eleven, they were paid for their labor.

As our discussion went on, it became clear that one of the reasons they were living there was the isolation, which protected the young folks from the dangers present in the wider world. They were creating a context for themselves and their children, in which relationships and experiences would be limited by their location at a wide spot on a winding hillside road, three miles from the nearest village.

The parents, of course, had a broader context in which to assess their lives. The father had other business interests, and the mother created a variety of beauty products using vanilla.

Several years ago, China expanded the context for this family. The Chinese created a twenty-acre vanilla farm, driving down the world price for vanilla. Globalization took its toll on family resources.

The father was a descendent of Mennonite settlers who had immigrated to Alberta, Canada, and later settled in British Columbia. When he was fifteen, his father had moved to the islands. Warm sun beats snow and ice.

The kids knew all this, not because they lived it, but because it was part of family history. They were being protected from the evils and temptations of modern life.

Then China — not dope, booze, or sex — intruded on their lives and threatened their security. The context within which they would be making decisions had suddenly expanded.

We all live in one world, but its size and shape differ for each of us. In the same way, my snorkeling has been altered by global climate change and loss of ocean reefs. As with the vanilla-farming family, the larger global context may be serving to destroy the smaller, more personal context in which I find great enjoyment.

FEAR AND THE FUTURE

There's a lot of speculation these days about "angry Americans," as the great debate on medical care continues. We can see them berating their legislators at town hall meetings designed to probe the public support for systemic medical reform.

The pictures we see suggest that, in the main, the angry protesters are white and middle-aged and beyond. They attack various proposals, such as federal medical care as opposed to private medical insurance, establishing so-called "death panels," federal funding for abortion, and anything that seems to change the medical care system as it currently exists.

Since this legislative process was begun by President Obama, he has become a focal point for some of the protests. This has given rise to analysts who shift the anger scenario away from health program issues and onto racism. The analysts suggest that these folks have never gotten over the fact that we elected an African American president.

Perhaps the animosity being displayed expresses something other than displeasure at a particular program proposal or racial prejudice. Beneath the anger, there may be a deep-seated fear of a new world beyond the control of individual Americans — and of America itself.

The issues confronting the president on inauguration day were part of every American's experience, either directly or through the mediation of the media. Print, video, Internet: all provided news and opinions about the recession, joblessness, enormous federal spending and deficits, two wars, and global warming. Joe Six-Pack and his relatives could look at the list and feel powerless, unable to deal with any one of them, let alone the totality of them.

Can we trust government to deal with them successfully? Poll data reveal that, into the 1970s, the majority of Americans trusted government to do the right thing most of the time. Ronald Reagan provided the *coup de grâce* for faith in government with his one-liner: "Government is not a solution to our problem, government is the problem."

Again, political polls indicate a general trust of the president himself, while doubts surround his various policies.

And the unease, anger, fear, or whatever the salient emotion is, becomes complicated by the rapidity of the changes we are all living through. It seems as though, every week or so, there is some new scientific or technological breakthrough that can have a significant impact on our lives.

My father lived from 1898 to 1977. He went from the horse and wagon to a man on the moon; from a minimum of government in the life of the average citizen to Social Security and Medicare; from the telephone to radio to color TV. There were enormous social and economic changes in his lifetime, and he coped with them.

Can we do as well, as we try to work through the changing conditions we face in our struggle to live happy, successful lives? If fear becomes the dominant motive within the polity, we will choose solutions that will ultimately fail. Fear may open our eyes wide, but in the end it blinds us, for it too often precludes rationality. A fear-ridden society will be a destructive society that destroys itself.

Happy Fourth of July

Small-town America is a big thing. Poets and novelists have celebrated the virtues found there. Recently, Ms. Sarah Palin, the lamentable ex-vice presidential nominee, voiced her belief that small-town America is the real America.

My brother has lived a good part of his life near a small California town in the Sierras. We visit him and his wife once a year and get to observe some of life in a mountain village.

The town itself is in the midst of golf courses replete with fairway homesites. A great many of the residents in these developments are retired folks who enjoy the golf, the fishing, and the being away from the Bay Area or other megalopolises.

This year, we were there on the Fourth of July weekend. Fireworks, a simulated Civil War battle, and a parade were on the agenda in this small town.

We watched the fireworks on Friday night at a packed church parking lot. For forty-five minutes or so, the sky was filled with flashes of light and streaking rockets exploding. Good fun, enjoyed by those around us, with no signs of any hassles.

We skipped the battle on Saturday, because we had seen it before. Cannons and the attendant big booms, cavalry charges, wounded soldiers being treated by the medical corps, and other things military were on display. We felt it was entertaining, but that once was enough.

The parade provided the best peek into life as it is lived in this place. For local businesses — grocery and liquor stores, restaurants, service stations — this can make or break the entire year.

Tourists flooded the town, lining the parade route on Highway 89 well in advance of the marchers. In the park where we had plunked our chairs, there were booths providing food and drink — even margaritas — but many brought their own *ingestibles* with them.

Families, from grandparents to the stroller-bound, were there in abundance. People moved around to greet friends and renew acquaintances. Very lighthearted and social.

It was the Fourth, and many signified this by the clothing they chose to wear: women and girls in dresses decorated like flags; men and boys in star-spangled T-shirts; ladies with necklaces made with red, white, and blue stones; and for everyone, red, white, and blue hats and caps to ward off the sun.

About twenty minutes before the parade was to begin, the highway patrol closed the highway. Drivers had to find circuitous routes around the town.

The parade began about one o'clock, a mile or so from the spot where the announcer on the loudspeaker would identify the various groups and individuals — even the local congressman — as they came into view.

The participants included local notables, some businesses, high school bands (one from Reno), community organizations, fire and police services from a variety of districts in the vicinity, a professional marching band, vintage cars, and, at the end, stagecoaches propelled by horses from the local stable. The crowd and the earlier marchers were happy to see the horses at the end of the parade.

The old cars included collectors' items like a 1929 Model A, a 1940 Dodge Luxury Liner, and a 1950 Ford truck. There was even a lumber truck dating from the 1940s.

The parade was over in slightly more than an hour. Then, in a corner of the park in which we sat, the Ophir Prison Marching Band and Temperance Society performed a fifty-minute concert and comedy routine. Good music and jokes.

It was a fine day, with simple and down-to-earth fun for both the older folks and the kids. It was a celebration of the nation and of people coming together to enjoy themselves and their friends.

For these troubled times, it was an encouraging omen. Forget the bad news and, for at least a long weekend, have an old-fashioned good time.

Herb Caen as Prophet

For years, *San Francisco Chronicle* columnist Herb Caen referred to San Francisco as "Baghdad by the Bay." As a third-generation San Franciscan, I took this as a compliment to my city. Beautiful. Mysterious. Historically significant. Blending history with modernity. San Francisco was clearly a world-class place.

Unfortunately, the phrase seems to be more relevant today than when it was coined. Baghdad is much larger than San Francisco, but if you expand the city's geographic boundary to encompass the San Francisco Bay Area, you approach comparability.

Would Mr. Caen use the imagery today? Probably not, but daily reading of his former publication reveals an entirely new link between Baghdad and the City by the Bay.

Murder now ties Baghdad to the Bay Area, and each morning the *Chronicle* records the carnage from both locations. Not, mind you, that our number of dead equals theirs, but almost always, there are multiple murders to describe. Most of the slaughter here takes place in the major cities around the Bay — though San Jose, our largest city, has a low homicide rate.

As in Iraq, gangs play a major role in our killings. There, the gangs tend to be sectarian in nature; here, the principal gang identifications are based on ethnicity and social class — Asian, African American, and Latino — and most of the slaughter is intra-ethnic and takes place in economically deprived areas. For example, Latino gangs are often broadly grouped as Norteno or Sudeno, referring to the length of time they have lived in the United States. Killing members of the rival gang over turf seems to be de rigueur.

Another similarity in the two cities is that a term in prison seems to act as a recruiting or training tool. Recent stories from Iraq about prison conditions mirror the myriad reports about California's prisons and the prevalence of gang influence within them.

While Saddam Hussein was a murderous dictator who conducted massacres of his Kurdish and Shiite subjects, the state was orderly. There was nothing like the chaotic conditions existing today. He had the ability and the willingness to kill in the name of the state.

Democracies cannot use these autocratic methods. How does a democratic society maintain order and remain a democracy? Two approaches have proven to be useful.

In San Jose, the police maintain close relationships with the local community and the gangs that exist there. Other cities have adopted the idea that crime and violence increase as the local environment deteriorates. Graffiti is cleaned up quickly, run-down buildings are repaired, broken windows replaced. Community policing, often on foot, links law enforcement and neighborhood members.

Is this, then, the choice confronting us as we consider strategies for bringing peace to the Bay Area — total malign force applied viciously *or* generating a greater sense of community, including intolerance of anti-social behavior and a closer relationship with law enforcement?

Not too difficult a choice, it would seem. However, one should not ignore the middle and upper classes' willingness to tolerate violence as long as it doesn't affect them.

There may come a time when the annoying headline overwhelms the tolerance, and brute force takes over. *Baghdad by the Bay* in a later incarnation.

I Don't Understand

"There's this white Catholic priest doing a sermon in Obama's church and attacking Hillary because she's white. And last week the gay marriage thing. I don't understand; I just don't understand anymore." So says a sixty-plus white guy to three others of the same description.

As I walked away, it struck me how hard it is to understand the social changes that have taken place in the sixty to seventy-five years represented in our little gabfest. So much that we took for granted as we grew up has been cast aside.

There were all those assumptions about race that we didn't have to verbalize because we were white. Our superiority, our power, was reflected throughout society. A black or Mexican doctor? You'd have to search. A person of color as a CEO of a major corporation? A black player on a major league baseball team?

I went to four public schools in San Francisco and met no African American students. There was an Asian in the junior high school I attended. Our isolation reflected and reinforced our sense of entitlement.

We, the secure and educated middle class, didn't often use the N-word, though our jokes might display an unflattering view of nonwhites.

In our classroom discussions of race, we generally accepted our teachers' pleas for tolerance and acceptance of others. This, too, reinforced the underlying sense of our self-worth — for if we can grant acceptance, doesn't that speak to our power?

We learned to descry the actions of white Southerners as they expressed their racial bias in state and local laws. White-only water fountains, schools, public transit, and restaurants were simply reflections of the ignorance of Southerners.

What has happened since the 1950s (maybe since 1954 and Brown v. Board of Education) has been a breakdown in our separate and unequal coexistence with nonwhites in the USA. First the courts, then Congress, and the Executive Branch have helped create an America where we have to compete with folks we used to regard as somewhere below us — legally, socially, economically, and intellectually.

So how does my age group cope with these changes in our racial reality? We can count the ways. But how do we come to understand our changed status, which diminishes our perceived birthright?

If the above sequence of events created confusion concerning our racial attitudes, a similar trail can be pursued relative to white males' attitudes toward white women. Nonwhite females were there to be fantasized over, but not to be with in public. You'd expect to marry a white woman with a background similar to your own, and she would settle down to be a housewife and mother. She might go to work after the kids were grown. But increasingly, through the fifties and sixties, as more women went to college and entered professions, childcare became an option, as it had been for the Rosie the Riveters in World War II. The two-income family required men to reassess their attitudes in the face of a rising feminist tide. Today, women make up 58 percent of college undergraduates.

But, perhaps, the issue we older white males least understand is the new openness related to homosexuality and gay marriage.

Growing up in liberal San Francisco, we knew about Finnochio's, where men acting as women were in stage shows. We also knew about bars for "queers" and "dykes," but we were isolated from the worlds that these folks inhabited. We might go look, but we were entering forbidden territory. I knew a couple of guys in high school who, in groups, had beaten homosexuals and boasted about it.

How can we understand these continuing social revolutions? What wisdom do we, the wise, have to pass on to our grandchildren?

And here we confront another reversal in the social system we grew up in. Poll data shows conclusively that, on issues around race and sex, the young can be our teachers and attitude guides in living life today.

So talk to young folks. Then, when someone complains that he "just doesn't understand," you can say, "Well, I had a good talk with my granddaughter, and she told me..."

It's Like a Job

Baseball was once the American game. Of late, pro football and NASCAR have challenged for primacy, but who cares? They all offer a day in the sun, a hot dog, a cold beer, and the company of folks out for a pleasant afternoon or evening.

The games are entertaining and, for the real aficionados, a source of statistics, visions of great players making stellar plays, and endless arguments about this or that.

For everyone, there is the social side of the event — the people around you with whom you interact. The crowd itself, responding to events on the field, promotes engagement.

Anyone with the price of admission can go to a game, so you never know who will show up. Sometimes the diversity makes for interesting contrasts.

Before a recent Giants game, my friend began a discussion with two men — father and son — in the row in front of us. Because we were within range of foul balls drifting into the stands, my friend suggested that the young man in front of us could serve as our protector by catching anything that came close.

His father said, "Don't worry. He's in the military and his reactions are really quick."

It turned out that the young man was a master sergeant set to go back to Iraq on a second tour in two weeks. "So, what do you feel about that?" my friend Bill asked.

"It's tough. But it's like a job — you've got to do it," said the father.

"You've got to do it." Yes, you do, if you're there, and you get there these days as a volunteer member of the armed forces or as a part of the cadre of much better paid contractors who are also there.

Time was, not so long ago, that the *you* included a much broader grouping of American young people. The all-volunteer military limits the breadth of participation in two closely related ways. The men and, now, women who volunteer in no way reflect the demographics of the nation. The middle and upper classes (yes, we do have classes) are vastly underrepresented. In the same way, middle- and upper-class parents are not part of the anxious, and sometimes grieving, mothers and fathers watching the news from Iraq.

As I sat there at the ballpark and observed my new acquaintances, several thoughts disturbed me. First, how would I, as a father, feel if my son were to be on his way back to Iraq because he *"had a job to do"*? How could I rationalize the soldier's job with the now widely accepted view that our leaders in Washington, D.C., had not done their jobs? Who bears the greater responsibility — the leadership or the master sergeants?

No foul balls came our way, and the Giants blew another game, despite the good pitching provided by Matt Cain. So back home for a glass of wine, dinner, TV, and some reading.

But in the mail was the weekly edition of the *Washington Post*, taking me back to the afternoon's disturbing thoughts. The lead stories were focused on the failure of the D.C. types to provide adequate care for Iraq war veterans suffering from psychiatric problems. Horrific story after horrific story, detailing the troubles of former military personnel.

At this point, it occurred to me that, if our soldiers, sailors, and marines were more representative of the body politic, there would be an enormous public reaction, with an attendant political outcome, to the failure to provide care. Middle- and upper-class folks know how to play that game.

But then, would we even be in Iraq if all of us were called upon to contribute our children or even contribute our taxes to the war effort?

It had been a lovely day, except for those intrusions of reality. As I prepared for bed, I thought again of the master sergeant and wished that he had been able to grab a foul. He'd have accomplished his job on that sunny Wednesday.

It's Morning in America

There is, I have read recently, an important social fact revealed by the time of day in which you habitually take a shower.

Those of us who work at physically demanding jobs, such as laborers, farmers, or miners, shower when they come home or before bed. For office workers, bankers, politicians, educators, and others whose jobs have minimal physical exertion, the preferred time for personal cleansing is the morning, before work.

This is a kind of shorthand for social class. Poor and working-class folk need to wash off perspiration and dirt at the end of a day's labor. Denizens of the middle and upper echelons of our society have to prepare themselves to look and smell good for the personal interactions that make up their day.

In the two summers that I worked as a laborer, I showered as soon as I got home. (There was one exception I am sure of — after my first day using a pick and shovel, I came home and fell into bed.) Why shower in the morning before you had collected your daily ration of dirt and sweat?

The morning under the rushing water has been my *modus vivendi* for all of my adult working life. There were classes of sensitive teenagers to be taught. Parents to be placated. Colleagues to be collegial with. Higher-level bureaucrats to be reassured. Voters to be won over. Young educators to be sold on the leadership program I was managing.

Nothing in the above list suggests that these tasks are any easier than those demanding more of one's body. In fact, because of their indeterminate nature, there can be significant psychological wear and tear. When I dug trenches for a fence, it was done when it was done, and I moved on to the next task. The results of my daily encounters with students, parents, and educators were, most often, far less clear-cut than that trench.

Now, as a retired person, I have become more *ambi-showerist*. I do not hit the stall before my three-times-a-week tennis efforts. The shower becomes a midday phenomenon. The hot water beating on my poor old bod feels great and prepares me for lunch or a snack. Being clean provides both a psychological and a physical boost.

Of course, a worker-worker encased in the leftovers from labor is finishing the day and beginning his or her own personal-relationship time. The daily shower is a twofer as opposed to my morning *one-fer*.

In our knowledge-based economy, the morning shower types will be an expanding demographic that will demand the attention of politicians. The existing social class distinction between *a.m.-ers* and *p.m.-ers* will have increased importance among lawmakers at all levels. Some will glory in the enhanced power of the middle and upper classes and a permanent decline in the power of those south of the middle.

To end our unemployment crisis, it seems we need a lot more *p.m.* shower takers.

It's Tough Out There

Murder in America is big these days — not just single assassinations but multiple killings, sometimes involving family members (son kills mother, father, siblings); sometimes settling public grievances (cops, council members, bureaucrats shot dead); sometimes seemingly random (five killed in mall shootings). Five students were recently killed at Northern Illinois University by an ex-student. And there were many more in the last thirty days than are listed in the brief recitation above.

How do we explain all this slaughter?

Dysfunctional families. Anger at the irrational inactions of government. Potential robberies to relieve poverty or procure drugs. Rivalries among street gangs. The failure of schools to educate. Insufficient legal deterrence. Random anger directed at available targets. A culture gone mad.

On one level I don't give a damn what causes it. Let's shut it down. Put people away.

What I want to know, even need to know, is what is going wrong in what the politicians are quick to say is the greatest nation in the world.

Certainly there are the nutcases — isolated individuals wreaking vengeance, like the student in West Virginia who slaughtered over thirty of his schoolmates. The shooter was able to get guns even though he had been diagnosed with mental and emotional problems. Simple solution: make it more difficult for people to get guns legally. The remaining problem: eliminate illegal ways to get weapons.

There are more and more families under stress as we move through recession with consequent pressure on jobs and, with the subprime disaster, maintaining a home. Kids feel the pressure even if they aren't privy to what's causing it.

The schools work with disturbed and undermotivated youngsters who know that they need an education. But their knowledge goes way beyond that. They know that their chances of legally sanctioned success are minimal. The schools expect little of them in terms of academic achievement, just as society at large is ready to consign them to failure, lawlessness, and prison. But beyond that, the economy is not producing the kinds of jobs that provide entrée to upward mobility for the uneducated and unskilled.

Movement — South to North

There they are on Army Street (oops, it's now named Cesar Chavez). Then they appear again in those fertile fields alongside Highway 101. And still again as you go off the freeway in Encinitas near San Diego and turn right.

Men working and men looking for work. If you stop overnight at a motel or hotel or go to a restaurant, you find more of them.

They are here, and their presence is growing throughout the nation. As their numbers increase, so do their value and their indispensability to all of us.

The Latinos, Hispanics, Mexicans, Central-South Americans — choose your label — search for a better life has led them here. They have arrived with or without a legal imprimatur.

Estimates of the number of illegal immigrants in the country hover around the twelve million mark. What to do about them is a policy question confronting the federal government — and the candidates striving for the Republican and Democratic parties' nominations for president.

The extremes of the proposals vary: deport them and then allow them to apply for legal admission, or find a way to keep them here with a chance to gain citizenship after they meet certain requirements.

As one who believes in the rule of law, I think governmental policies that subvert the law would be counterproductive. There should be a penalty for lawbreakers. Yet deporting twelve million people brings to mind Nazi cattle cars loaded with Jews. The answer must lie elsewhere.

One step toward an answer would be to make serious attempts at involving the Mexican government in working with us to develop a joint approach. This would be difficult because the illegals relieve the pressure of unemployment on the Mexican economy and send millions of dollars every year back to their families.

However this problem is solved, resolved, or just lived with, we know that there is a real social, cultural, and economic rationale for us gringos to perfect our Spanish. It's a lovely language and provides a first step in understanding another culture and its people, especially as they become not *them* but *us*.

Shaken or Stirred?

The numbers are discouraging enough. Over 8 percent unemployment nationwide; over 10 percent in California. Another half million plus Californians without medical insurance. More thousands of foreclosures. Another number: in Contra Costa County, 36 percent of families are living with incomes that barely meet their basic needs.

But the numbers in the paper don't begin to tell the story or to hint at what is really going on. We got a better (maybe it should be worse) feel for it last night.

On our way to dinner with some friends, we drove down Highway 101 (called the Bay Shore in a less number-infatuated world) to San Mateo. As we moved along, we could see, on our right, building after building advertised as vacant. Off to the left, we spotted several more. These buildings once housed workers — people producing and selling things. Now they were empty, and the workers were gone.

Our destination was a very good and not terribly expensive restaurant in San Mateo. We arrived about six and were the only customers in the place. About five minutes later, a couple came in and took a table across the dining room. We left after seven fifteen. Our two fellow diners were still there. No other patrons had come through the door.

There have been numerous recessions in the United States since World War II — seven that I can count. Our current predicament is the most severe, combining an economic slowdown with a worldwide financial crisis generated, in large part, by bad economic and regulatory policies in the United States.

O woe is us, for the straits they are dire!

But wait — President Obama, following the theories of British economist John Maynard Keynes, is attempting to stimulate the economy with a huge program of deficit spending designed to produce jobs and put people back to work. Unemployment is a more serious issue in America than in Western Europe because their social safety nets are much stronger than ours — theirs include more liberal unemployment benefits and national health care systems. They're spending, but it's built into their existing benefit regulations.

Among the twenty largest economies there is broad agreement on new regulations designed to prevent or limit future financial crises. Each nation will develop a program responsive to its own political system.

We are lucky because, at this time, we have a government that believes in government and that is willing to act. The previous administration was ideologically opposed to government action and was populated with antigovernment bureaucrats at its upper levels.

It was bizarre. A bunch of people who were opposed to something were hired to make it work. Would any bar put a bunch of prohibitionists behind the plank to mix Bloody Marys?

Maybe government policies and actions, carried out in the belief that they can actually work, will not be enough to get us through our economic travail. What we know is that government inaction and errant policy played a major role in the debacle the Obama administration inherited.

Our hopes ride on the new guys serving up the drinks.

Skills and Will

It's a political year, and one way I follow the ins and outs, the lies and truths of the sport is via MSNBC, which advertises itself as the place for political news.

That's not all there is on this channel. It's ironic that when they're not covering the political scene, the MSNBCers are doing stuff on prisons and, in many cases, criminals who have lost the right to vote.

On occasion, I have turned to channel 60 a bit too early for some of the politics, and I have seen an advertisement for a prison flick. Checking the schedule in the newspaper reveals that this is a continuing phenomenon.

So, after watching the Spaniards win the European soccer championships against the Germans, I noticed in the TV guide that San Quentin, our local state prison, was to be featured on good old channel 60. So, since it's local (and I need an excuse for my actions), I tuned in.

An interviewer and his camera operator spent time talking with some convicts while showing some of their life within — repetitive, boring, and resigned. The program covers only level two prisoners. Each man is rated one to four, with four being the most dangerous. Two is safer.

It is clear that these inmates, even those rated two, who play baseball and tennis or create art, have done evil things.

Yes, there is evil, and there are evil people. So we have a system of laws and enforcement to deter evil actions. Then there are punishments that are supposed to fit the crime. Minor offenses equal fines, probation, or brief incarceration in a city or county jail. Conviction for murder can result in the death penalty.

There are currently 1.6 million people locked up in America's prisons and jails. It costs between $30,000 and $40,000 a year to keep someone behind bars. In California, those awaiting execution reside on death row, where the expense jumps to $90,000 per year just for the housing. There are other attendant expenses that boost the amount by more than $80,000 per annum per death-row inhabitant.

All of the above is meant to highlight the enormous price we pay for punishing evildoers. And, as noted, we generate a goodly number of them.

So three questions pop into my old mind: Why are we, as a nation, so successful at producing villains? What are the true costs — actual expenditures, plus socially beneficial projects not undertaken for lack of funds? Are there effective alternatives to the punishment system we utilize now?

We know that vast numbers of our felons are barely literate and come from deprived backgrounds. These victimizers are also victims who lack access to the American mainstream. Their hopes for the future — when they have hope — are often tied to success in illegal activities. Their need for acceptance is expressed in their gang memberships, where they find people in situations similar to their own.

Criminal gangs of young men and women, often formed around ethnic or national identity, have become more and more powerful and dangerous. We know we cannot lock them all up or deport them wholesale. Even if we put them away, many will come out of prison as greater menaces to society than when they entered prison.

Crime is expensive in terms of property and lives stolen. Together, crime and the costs associated with bringing criminals to justice and putting them away carry a significant price. We seemingly lack the ability to solve the crime problem in America. Or maybe it's our unwillingness to address, or even expose, the myriad factors involved in American criminality.

When John F. Kennedy challenged our scientists to put a man on the moon, the task was accepted and accomplished. We had rocket scientists who could do the job and a public willing to pay for it.

Do we have the scientific skills and the political will to take on the crime issue in the same way we did with our moon venture? The odds are against it. The candidates won't touch it.

THEIR FAITH, MY FEAR

Dear Sir,

Faith. It scares me. Probably because I don't have a lot, except in the little things, like family and the general sense that more people want to do good rather than evil.

It's the bigger kinds of faith that scare me, like "I speak with God"; "I have a God-sanctioned mission"; "I believe I know the right and the truth"; and "I ask you to have faith in my faith."

Okay. But am I allowed to express a few doubts? Good, then I will.

At some point, faith — yours, mine, everyone's — gets tested. Faith seems to imply some implicit or explicit outcomes, which believers will experience. Maybe it's the promise of life everlasting or faith that the brakes will function. But you ask me to have faith in you, and you tell me that — if I have faith long enough — what you say will happen, happens.

The problem. You have said that many times, and you have been wrong many times. When you were proven wrong, you never acknowledged that you were wrong. You only made another promise about the desired outcome and asked us to accept the new vision. When you could not fulfill your promise, you blamed me for my lack of faith in your vision, and so it became my error, not yours, that prevented the fulfillment of your promise.

But sir, enough is enough. While you may impugn all those with little faith, it is those who maintain their faith in your faith

41

who are squandering lives and treasure in pursuit of whatever it is you are pursuing, whether in foreign lands or here at home.

Now the press is full of stories about yet another military adventure being planned. The fear campaign, precedent to your use of force, is functioning. The way out of the fear is through faith in force and in your direction of that force.

Einstein said, "Insanity is doing the same thing over and over again and expecting different results." If you keep asking me to have faith in your faith and the results are always negative, only insanity would compel such faith from me.

No. The time has come to test out some old ideas that, over several centuries, have earned our respect — the rule of law, the constitution and its division of powers, and government "of the people, by the people, and for the people."

THE WAR UPON US

Americans have a difficult time talking about class — as opposed to *classy*, an adjective widely used and sought after to describe a person, a consumer product, or a lifestyle.

When it comes to social class, we are middle. Oh, there are some who see themselves as working class and others who might identify themselves as low income or even poor. But lower class? Never.

Even those who might seem to be upper class tend to think of themselves as the high end of the middle.

By accepting our *middleness* and avoiding the negativity of any other descriptors, we make it difficult for those potential leaders among us who, in their pursuit of power, could raise the specter of class warfare. That sort of stuff was found in the rigidities of Europe or in the emerging nations, with their narrow leadership groups exerting control over society.

While Americans have not seen their nation as classless, they pictured their society as fluid and mobile — a place where the average man's fate was not circumscribed by birth or economic status. We were, in our own minds, a land of becoming, where what we became was up to us.

The United States is a young nation, when viewed in the context of world history. Italy and Germany were created later than the United States, but their societies pre-dated the newcomer to the West. Youth is a time for naïveté, and perhaps that is the source of the dream that has marked us. *Yes we can* was a motto long before 2008.

A picture emerges of a young man or woman taken with the American Dream. As part of the middle class, he or she desired the good life, and, given the country's wealth, they often achieved success and comfort. Class and class warfare made no sense.

So the dreamers and their descendent dreamers dream on, becoming consumers. Buyers of goods and services. The good times roll on, justifying the dream.

The leaders of the nation, the elected officials and the movers and shakers of the economy — that is, the powerful upper class — create new seductive schemes to make consuming easier. Easy credit and flexible payment plans for purchasing homes become available, even for those who cannot afford them.

But then, in October 2008, the seduction ends with shattered dreams and recriminations. The vast middle, primary victims of the seducers, demand vengeance as their comforts disappear. Their anger intensifies as they see those who took advantage of their innocence reaping enormous financial gains.

Now class warfare has meaning, but it is not the classic uprising of the poor and downtrodden against the powerful.

It is the powerful who have waged war against the weak, seducing them and then abandoning seduction for rape.

Throughout history, the powerful have been able to take advantage of those below them on the power ladder. It was expected — except when the society's motivating dream held that all had access to power and the good life.

As the bosses at Goldman Sachs, perhaps the most powerful of the financial powers in the United States, appeared before a senate committee, they glibly admitted they had made mistakes. They accepted responsibility for their mistakes. They vowed to be more careful in the future. They did *not* propose to return the outlandish bonuses they had awarded themselves in recent years.

A recent article in *Newsweek,* written by Stephen Green, Chairman of HSBC Bank, explores a different sort of responsibility that the affluent should accept in return for the power they wield. He suggests that the affluent should give back by giving and donating their time and talents.

This is a far broader responsibility than that accepted by the Goldman boys. And while it reads like some kind of paternalism or *noblesse oblige*, it proposes a new focus and new behaviors for those who have earned our distrust.

It is time they travel the road less traveled and earn our forgiveness and respect.

TOWARD BEING A CITIZEN

A long time ago — over sixty years — I was confirmed in the Lutheran Church. To reach that state, I had to take part in a series of classes and then, with my classmates, participate in a question-and-answer session led by our minister.

I immodestly admit that I was a star at the quizzing. My hand was constantly waving, indicating I knew the answer to the question asked. Just like in eighth-grade U.S. history.

What no one but me knew was that my knowledge came, not from the classes or from hours of study, but from a radio series based on stories from the Bible. I had regularly listened to the program when I had been ill and housebound.

The confirmation marked a rite of passage. I was now a member of the church, no longer just an attendee at Sunday School. Throughout history, religions, cultures, social groups — even families — have created ceremonial occasions to mark a person's coming of age.

Another such rite in the USA — and for some, the most important signification of maturity — is the acquisition of a driver's license. The state bestows this upon those who have attained a specific age and passed some tests.

Now what in the world brought all this stuff to mind? As near as I can tell, the *precipitator* — if Bush can be *decider*, then it's OK for there to be a *precipitator* — was a mention of our grandson, who will be entering high school in September. He is in the final years of his march to maturity. (Our daughter has had another type of coming of age experience recently — an invitation to join AARP.)

Or grandson has no experience with an organized religion, so confirmation is not available to him — or millions of others who are in a similar situation. What can we do for these folks that will symbolize, for them and others, their new status?

Aha, says I. We can confirm them as citizens in the same manner that I was confirmed a Lutheran — with a test. A citizenship test. We do that already for immigrants who want to become citizens, so why not extend the idea beyond its current box?

And we could add a second part to the process: voting. All who pass the written or oral test would be required to vote at the next election.

The test could include a variety of true-or-false and multiple-choice questions and one essay centered upon a significant issue confronting the nation. For example:

True or False

1. *Congress can declare war.*
2. *All members of the House of Representatives must be born in the United States.*
3. *The Constitution mandates that education is a state responsibility.*

Multiple Choice

1. *If the president and vice president die or are incapable of performing their duties, who succeeds to the presidency?*

a) *The Secretary of State*
b) *The Speaker of the House*
c) *The Chairperson of the National Security Council*

2. *If the Supreme Court rules a law passed by Congress and signed by the president unconstitutional, Congress may do what?*

a) *Pass a law vetoing the Court's decision*
b) *Pass a law correcting the problem cited by the Court*
c) *Challenge the Court's decision*

3. *The president*

a) *Is guaranteed a four-year term*
b) *May be removed from office by a vote of the House of Representatives*
c) *Can be elected only twice*

Essay

List and discuss three foreign policy issues confronting the nation today.

On second thought, let's forget it. Those of us born here are born citizens. So birth is our rite of passage. We have the right to vote and participate in our politics, but maybe, like the Australians and the citizens of over twenty-five other countries, we should be mandated to vote and fined if we don't do it.

Now if we'd only vote the right way.

Truth, What Do You Do with It?

The truth, 'tis written, *shall make you free*. Recently, I found out that it can also make you angry, disappointed, and a bit fearful.

About the 'tis part: the 1980 edition of *Bartlett's Familiar Quotations* lists 366 quotes centered on truth, with the one above originating in the Bible's Gospel according to John and, therefore, with a religious reference which we shall ignore here.

Truth is, by hand-count, an important item. The *make you free* part is open to question.

Recently, my friend Al noted, in the midst of a semi-political discussion, that he was "never going to watch *60 Minutes* again." His newfound resolution — he was only a now-and-then viewer — was his reaction to a *60 Minutes* story on the interface between politicians and money, or doing the people's business and lobbying. It seems a congressman who had headed a committee devoted to oversight of the drug industry had recently become a lobbyist for that very same industry.

I am not attempting here to equate *60 Minutes* with "the truth" — they have strayed from that line on occasion (Dan Rather and Bush's military records, for example). This, however, was factual stuff, which implied that the congressman's link to the drug industry, as one of its overseers, had (a) been compromised and (b) led to his post-congressional employment.

After announcing his commitment to a *60 Minutes*–free life, my friend went on to voice his anger at the show for revealing the kind of relationship some of us view as simply the way things are, and at the former legislator for his activities both observable and implied.

In essence, Al was PO'd that *60 Minutes* had told him what he didn't want to hear, truthful or not. It was clear, too, that his anger reflected disappointment at the workings of "the system" that had made the ex-lawmaker a millionaire.

I, on the other hand, was neither angry nor disappointed by the story. I had seen the same program and had enjoyed the segment that had generated Al's reaction. *So what else is new?* I might have thought. *It's gone on forever.*

So one bit of truth and two very different reactions. What's to make of it?

Al will attempt to shield himself from other unpleasant truths in hopes he won't be discomfited. Momentary anger and disappointment, leading inevitably to the freedom not to know.

My blasé acceptance of the reality portrayed did not signify approval of this behavior. Rather, it was my acceptance of the norm — a certain amount of it was expected, but it needed to be dealt with and not ignored.

Expectations, we are told by psychologists and sociologists, trigger behavior. If you expect people to behave badly, they will meet your expectations. We are told to "raise our kids' expectations" for achievement. Teams that expect to win have a better chance of winning.

So I, with my low-key expectation for crooked behavior, am actually promoting it, and this leads me to fear the emotion I felt as I thought about Al and my response to the story. The fear had two sides. First, how many people faced with what they don't want to know will decide to exercise their freedom not to know? Second, how many others will view the situation as I did and not as the outrage it is?

We can take guidance in affairs like this from Patrick Henry: "For my part, whatever anguish of spirit it may cost, I am willing to know the whole truth, to know the worst and to provide for it."

WE CAN AFFORD US

It was a difficult phone call to make. We were to go out to dinner with some friends when something went wrong with my wife's left knee. A painkiller didn't help, so dinner was postponed. The day before, I woke up with much more than the usual pain in my back and my right leg from my chronic sciatica. Doing my exercises didn't help. Today it's OK.

We are told this stuff is to be expected as we grow older. *Newsweek* magazine's Robert Samuelson wrote recently that one third of the nation's two-trillion-dollar health care bill goes for treating those sixty-five and older. The AARP should adopt a new slogan: *Health care is us.*

As I think about it, that one third seems like it could be a bit low. Among friends and family, there have been the following medical procedures in the last year or so: back surgery, hip replacement, a new knee, pacemaker implantation, and multiple cataract operations, as well as treatments for stroke, Lou Gehrig's disease, and shoulder dysfunction — not to mention the tons of pills we consume per annum.

This crisis in old folks' care has come of age. Growing up, I knew only one person over sixty-five (the retirement age chosen, in part, because not many people lived that long). Now over one-eighth of the United States is beyond sixty plus five.

Are we supposed to feel guilty because we have lived too long? Are we expected to give up whatever federal or insurance coverage we have to pay for our medical problems? Maybe we should find that mythical iceberg and float away to our chilly demise. I say, *no!* to all of the above.

Other industrial societies face similar issues, and, in a variety of international studies, they provide better medical care to their citizens than we do. Check their life expectancy rates and infant mortality. Oh, and look at the relative costs — in the United States vs. France, Germany, the United Kingdom, and Canada.

It is clear that our medical system needs to be rethought. There are over forty-five million of us who have no medical coverage beyond the federal program for the very poor or the emergency room. Those other industrial nations have developed a variety of ways to provide medical care to all their citizens.

If we do remake the ineffectual mélange we call health care, it will cost taxpayers. But there are other expensive programs we seem to put up with. How about 1.6 trillion dollars for a foolish, illegal, and mistaken war in Iraq?

I really don't like the idea of floating around on that iceberg.

WELCOME TO THE USA

Every once in a while, the great issues of the day intrude into my retirement life, and it has happened again.

Recently, we had some work done on our kitchen. There was a long process of interviewing contractors and sorting bids, and finally my wife came up with her approved duo — one to handle the cabinets, another to put in granite countertops throughout the kitchen.

Nice guys, hard workers, fluent speakers of Spanish. They had come with splendid recommendations, and they lived up to them.

We did not question them as to their nations of origin or their legal status. Our cabinet guy volunteered in a conversation that he was from Guatemala and had been here for thirty years. He has a daughter in medical school and a son in art school.

So? I didn't think much about it. This is California, the immigrant capital of the United States. People come here to work and improve their ways of life. Their kids go on to school just like the progeny of previous immigrants. Then I got an invitation in the mail.

While an undergraduate at UC Berkeley, I had been invited to join a university-sponsored group called The Order of the Golden Bear. As a senior, I went to a couple of meetings and then, after graduating, forgot about it for 363 days a year. Twice per annum came an invitation to attend the induction of new members. A quick glance and into the circular file.

This August, I read through the list of new members. Bingo — back to the guy from Guatemala and his children. Of the nineteen initiates, there were seven surnames that I could place as European in derivation. It was an extraordinary mélange of names from a variety of continents. In my head, without doing any checking and probably because I, like the Guatemalan, had bought into the American dream, I saw this list as proof that the dream is alive.

And the kitchen really looks great.

What's the Problem?

It's the end of a lovely afternoon at the ballpark. We just saw a close, well-pitched game that the Giants lost. We hurriedly leave the stadium to catch the train to Millbrae.

Reaching the station, we find the cars crowded, with standing room only, so we hustle ourselves up the platform to the car immediately behind the engine. As we climb the five stairs, we can see that this car, too, is packed.

Gently shoving the people ahead of me, I seek a space where I can hold on to the back of a seat or the supports of the second deck. As I look, something brushes against my legs. Glancing down, I see a slender seven- or eight-year-old boy crawling on the floor amidst the legs and feet surrounding him. He slowly moves his body around so that he is in a sitting position, blocking the aisle. His father, or someone minimally in charge of him, tells him to get up.

The head goes down, and a whine comes up. Then the face lifts to reveal a petulant, pained expression, denying his father's request. Then comes a command, and an arm grabs him by the shoulder. He rises halfway and then squirms back to the floor. As I and several others watch, he reaches into the backpack on the floor, pulls out the Giants' program booklet, turns around so he is sitting again, and begins to read.

You get the picture — the car filled with standees, including the father. The kid and the backpack on the floor, blocking any movement, and the train underway.

Daddy tries once again. Same results. We get to San Bruno, where some people get off, and new folks get on. The kid moves a bit to avoid being stomped, but he is still there on the floor. Poor Dad looks pained.

And I am piqued. In fact, my pique peaks as we near Millbrae and make ready to get off the train. I lean down and, in a somewhat reasonable voice, tell him, "Get up, you're blocking the aisle."

Kid looks at Dad. Dad looks at kid. Nothing happens.

I move carefully to the doorway, avoiding his little body while wanting to somehow tell him — and most importantly, Mr. Ineffective — that they are irresponsible, thoughtless, and very lucky. What if the train got involved in an accident? Or, more likely, what if someone tripped on the child or inadvertently stepped on or kicked him? Injuries directly related to parental incompetence would have occurred.

Now, I ask myself, why does this little incident make me so angry? Probably my own impotence in the situation. But I am not alone — nobody else did anything, even though they showed by their expressions that they disapproved of what was going on.

Perhaps, though, it was just the inability or unwillingness of that parent to correct and keep his child safe that irked me.

In the end, it was just a minor incident marring a splendid day. So pour another glass of wine — I'll simmer down in time for Jon Stewart.

Yes, We Can

In another essay, I comment upon the ethnic diversity I noticed among the staff at the local Kaiser Foundation Hospital.

Several weeks after that observation, I got a much closer look at this phenomenon. I was admitted to the hospital for an out-patient surgical procedure to remove a noncancerous growth on my head. Consequently, I found myself in the hands of the whole wide world. Herewith, a look at that world:

- The admitting nurse — Anglo
- The nurse who processed my admission papers — Latino
- The nurse who took my temperature and blood pressure — Filipino
- The nurses who assisted in the surgery — two Japanese and two Anglos
- The anesthesiologist — Jewish American
- The surgeon — African American
- The post operation — an Asian of undetermined national background
- Other professional staff observed and noted — four or five probably Filipinos, four African Americans, four Anglos, and three Latin Americans

I lay on my bed, prior to being wheeled into surgery, and marveled at the ways in which these folks operated as a team, with the five or six patients waiting for the operating room. Several months ago, the hospital began to utilize a new computerized program for keeping and displaying patient records. Some of the staff were still learning the process; others, who were more familiar with it, responded quickly when a colleague had a question.

When not working with patients, the nurses and other staff conversed in a relaxed manner and seemed to enjoy one another's company. I remembered the plaintive cry of Rodney King, "Can't we all get along together?"

Yes, we can. And the lesson may lie in the fact that the professionals I had observed shared responsibility for their patients, and they were all on display together in that large room near the surgery.

Getting along together may be easier when another overriding consideration forces us to depend on one another. Working and living together in a diverse nation is, if the immigration numbers from around the world are to be believed, the twenty-first century.

By building on examples like the South San Francisco Kaiser Hospital, we may well put ourselves in an advantageous position so that we may become, once again, a model for the world.

POLITICS

I've been involved in politics for over sixty years. I began by handing out campaign literature for a candidate my dad supported. He won, and I was hooked. I majored in political science at Berkeley but still retained my family's Republican orientation until 1960. Nixon for president? No, thanks. Since then, I have walked precincts, written press releases, and given speeches for Democratic candidates. In the 1970s, I won the first of four successful campaigns for our local school board. As a geezer, I follow the game closely. It's ugly out there now.

Leadership and Responsibility?

I've been around — not much in terms of the age of the earth, but a goodly assortment of days and nights. So there have been a lot of things I've seen and done. In some ways, I've become a bit blasé about the latest events depicted on the twenty-four-hour news cycle. People will, of course, be people.

But just the other day, I found out that my mother and a host of others who told me how to behave when I was growing up were hopelessly idealistic and out of current fashion. It all involves one word — responsibility.

"You've got to accept responsibility for what you do," my mother would preach as I tried to avoid blame for some mistake I had made.

"In a democracy, the citizens are responsible for making it work," the teachers intoned endlessly in high school history and civics classes.

"Don't drink and drive — act responsibly," we were told by college deans and counselors.

And, of course, it was a given that marriage brought forth new levels of responsibility.

In some ways, responsibility is like a big-league batting average. Nobody bats 1,000 or even .500, and nobody behaves responsibly all the time. But in the responsibility league, you should do better than a .230-hitting shortstop making a million dollars a year.

So, as in most things, perfection is beyond us. There are times, in an assessment, when we fall short in the responsible behavior category. Yet I have always believed that the goal is always there for most of us — we want to be held accountable for our actions and be responsible human beings.

How, then, do we account for the failure of our national leaders, those we have elected or their minions, who refuse to accept responsibility for actions and events that are, by law or by job description, within their realm of activity? Not only do some duck responsibility, they seem to seek out fall guys to take the heat when things go wrong.

The conviction of Lewis "Scooter" Libby surfaced the responsibility issue. One of the jurors, a spokesperson for the jury, said in an interview with the press, "Libby was the fall guy. He was tasked by the vice president to go and talk to reporters." He did as he was apparently instructed, and lied to a grand jury and the FBI.

Libby was found guilty, but what about those who made him the fall guy while they avoided responsibility? I've always believed that the moral tone in an organization starts at the top. Somebody decides and models acceptable behavior within the structure.

Since over 40 percent of eligible voters in this nation don't vote, maybe we're getting what we deserve.

LEADERSHIP

This is a day of national consecration, and I am certain my fellow Americans expect that on my induction into the presidency I will address them with a candor and a decision, which the present situation of our nation impels. This is preeminently the time to speak the truth, the whole truth, frankly and boldly. Nor need we shrink from honestly facing conditions in our nation today. This great nation will endure as it has endured, will revive, and will prosper.

The statement above will not be a part of Inauguration Day 2009, but we can hope that the call for an honest assessment of the conditions facing the nation will be a hallmark of the next White House inhabitant.

Franklin D. Roosevelt's principal concern in his first inaugural address, quoted above, was the depression that had crippled the American economy. He had to deal with rising rates of unemployment; a financial meltdown forcing the closure of banks; and what pundits today would call "a crisis of confidence." That was what he confronted in 1933.

If President 44 chooses to speak "the truth, the whole truth," will that be sufficient to address the anxieties — even fears — that permeate a significant portion of our body politic?

It would be easy to lay out a list of what afflicts us: Iraq, medical care, the subprime mortgage thing, offshoring of jobs, etc., etc., etc. There is stuff in the air that, like the smog in some of our major cities, obscures our view and, at the same time, seems a portent of our future. Some of the stuff floating around is ever-present in the media and, through casual conversation, produces more anxiety than understanding.

- The *Washington Post National Weekly* recently ran a story titled "The Can't Do Nation," referring to the perceived decline of the United States from a "can do" ethic to a "can't do" reality.
- TV and newspapers report that the U.S. military cannot account for 190,000 weapons it has shipped to Iraq.
- *National Geographic, Newsweek,* and other periodicals publish lengthy reports on the global warming phenomenon, supporting Al Gore's award-winning film on the same subject.
- A well-credentialed financial advisor, talking to an eighth-grader about the stock market, warns him that this current generation of kids will have a more difficult financial future than their parents or grandparents.
- American travelers find out that the once mighty dollar has lost substantial value over the past several years.
- Graphic pictures and stories about the American infrastructure crisis proliferate in all the information-dispensing media.
- Perhaps most important for the incoming chief executive is the general feeling that we as a nation are going the wrong way and that our government is unwilling or unable to handle the situation.

In politics, truth often depends upon the ideological stance of the perceiver and teller of the particular truth. Yet today, there appears to be enough agreed-upon paranoia in the public to give Number 44 the freedom to delineate the issues confronting the nation and develop proposals for dealing with them. If not, we may well face the future that Roosevelt was striving to avoid:

> *So first of all let me assert my firm belief that the only thing we have to fear is fear itself — nameless, unreasoning, unjustified terror, which paralyzes needed efforts to*

convert retreat into advance. In every dark hour of our national life, a leadership of frankness and vigor has met with that understanding and support of the people themselves, which is essential to victory.

FDR proceeded to propose, and the Congress approved, a series of policies to address the recession. Action followed from the words. Not everything worked, and there were ups and downs in the economy, but the government was acting. Whoever gets to be 44 has a lesson plan to follow.

An Exercise in Punditry

An election doth make pundits of us all, whether appearing on TV, radio, the Internet, or at the barber shop — the preferred habitat for the quadrennial pundit, a not-so-rare bird who is always with us but flourishes during presidential election time.

They are a mighty flock, enhanced in recent years with significant numbers of males and females of multitudinous colors. Of late — the last three days — the flock has adopted a uniform song. *Changes* they sing in baritone or soprano, in liberal or conservative. *Change* is what the electorate is voting for.

What is less clear than the call for change is what we are going to change to. Here it would appear (pardon the pending punditry) that Democrats have the advantage. For them, change is moving Republicans out of decision-making roles and Democrats taking their place.

For Republicans to chase after change suggests there is something wrong with them as the current holders of the *decidership*. "Reelect us, and we promise to do better than we have — not that we've done anything wrong. You know you can't trust them (the Democrats) to handle the job. So stick with us."

It will be interesting to observe Republican candidates on the couch, confronting, avoiding, and denying their party's culpability for the abysmal situation the nation faces today.

From the beginning of the campaign (sometime in the long, long ago, it seems), some candidates have chosen to differentiate themselves from the administration on specific issues.

Ron Paul emphasizes getting out of Iraq and controlling spending and the size of government.

John McCain has had problems with management of the Iraq war but supports the *Surge*. He's also opposed some Bush tax cuts.

Mike Huckabee proposes a much more activist government, relative to the problems of the poor.

Mitt Romney has had mild criticisms.

Fred Thompson proposes a different tax strategy.

Rudy Giuliani says he'll do more of the same — only better.

Of the six, Huckabee, a populist (meaning he cares about the poor), and Paul, a libertarian (meaning he opposes government), present the starkest contrasts to the incumbency. In fact, Huckabee is being attacked with great gusto by many of the economic conservatives who support his party.

For the Democrats, there is some kind of unanimity about medical care. Iraq is a problem for them, but all want to get us out and to emphasize diplomacy and multilateral approaches to foreign policy. The deteriorating economy will play into their hands in the general election, and today they agree on the need to strengthen the middle class.

Barack Obama's notion of change appears to be more focused on attitudes and the importance of coming together as a nation. John Edwards blasts away at corporate America and the evils it has brought. Hillary Clinton paradoxically purveys her experience and the need for change.

And now for punditry. The decisive issues in November 2008, will be Iraq and the Middle East — why, how, and when to get out. On the domestic side, the economic health of the nation will be big. On one side will be those who favor government policies to assist the middle class and the poor. Economic conservatives will take the position that protecting corporate profits is key to economic resurgence, and making the Bush tax cuts permanent is one policy approach.

Another issue that has been underplayed in the media and is code-word-laden in the campaign is the role of science and religion in governmental policymaking. This could be a dramatic conflict.

Perhaps the biggest bat in the Democrats' bat rack is competence. The outs can blast away at the incumbent displays of incompetence (early Iraq, Katrina, Gonzales, and so forth). The Republicans will be hard put to prove they have shown themselves competent at governing.

See, anyone can do it. All it takes is a bit of arrogance.

Election 2008

David Gergen. Remember him? Over a twenty-plus-year period, he worked for four presidents. He played conservative to Mark Shields' liberal on the *MacNeil-Lehrer News Hour* — a serious political commentator not given to good guy/bad guy thinking.

Gergen spoke a couple of nights ago to about five hundred people, most of whom were either drawing social security checks or would be doing so in a year or two. He defined himself as being in that age group.

It was a terrific presentation. Good funny stories. Informed political commentary. And, best of all, a sense of hope for the future.

Story! A guy is walking down a road and sees a frog. Frog looks up and says, "Kiss me, and I'll turn into a beautiful woman."

Guy picks up frog and puts it in his pocket. Frog says, "Hey man, didn't you hear me?"

"Yeah, I did, but at my age I'd rather have a talking frog."

Political commentary! The first year of the next president's term will be extraordinarily difficult for whichever Republican or Democrat wins.

Hope! Both parties are talking about change, and their talk links to events and trends already underway in the society. Young people — under forty — are proving to be daring and innovative.

Throughout his one-hour presentation and his thirty-minute Q&A, there were numerous loud outbursts of applause. As we left, there was animated discussion among the attendees — and smiles, lots of smiles.

Change and hope — that's what the current campaign must be all about. The doo-doo we are in is deep and getting deeper.

There are those candidates whose basic message is fear laden. "Elect me, and I will protect you." But most send a message that says, "We can do it." With strong emphasis on the *we*. Not just a narrowly based *we*, but something like the World War II *we*, when FDR called upon Republicans to take key positions in his cabinet.

Getting to *we* will not be easy. Deep divisions have arisen in our national political life, precluding the easy social camaraderie that marked the Reagan–Tip O'Neil relationship of the 1980s.

If we, the voting public, see the national economy as harmful to our best interests and therefore generate big Democratic majorities in both houses, along with a Democratic president, the job will be easier. If the new prexy has to work with a closely divided legislature, it will require Rooseveltian political skills to get anything done.

In the meantime, we watch the various horse races around the nation and begin to place our bets. The results will promote significant change in our government policies or permit only insufficient baby steps toward a largely undefined goal.

A recent issue of the magazine *Foreign Policy* had a picture of G. W. Bush on the cover. It proclaimed, "Don't blame him — it's our fault." Too true. Let us learn from our errors.

LIBERALISM

Idrive a Volvo. As a matter of fact, we have two Volvos. And while my wife is abstemious, I drink a goodly amount of chardonnay. Since 1968, I have marched to protest two wars. I have voted for tax increases to support education. I pay dues to the Democratic Party, the ACLU, and several environmental groups. I tend to vote the Democratic ticket in state and national elections. I label myself a liberal.

But labels can be deceptive. We have been told that when shopping for food we need to look beyond the label to check the ingredients. What are the chemical constituents of my liberalism? What are the beliefs that motivate my political actions? What is it I want?

My liberal values include the following: Equality of opportunity. Freedom of expression and belief. An open political system. Optimism. The need to safeguard our environment. The value of hard work. The importance of family. Effective and affordable education. The rule of law. The superiority of science, as opposed to ideology, in decision making. The existence of a common good. And so on.

A chapter or two in a political science text could be written in an attempt to operationalize the phrases above. It would probably be a pretty dull book. Let me try in one sentence to pull it together. I, the liberal (and to my knowledge most of those who accept that label), believe that we have it within our power to create a social system that will respond to the needs of its citizens for a secure and free life.

To achieve the above values, we believe that our governments (national, state, and local) can be helpful. We certainly do not exclude private sector involvement, initiative, and ingenuity in creating an economy capable of generating the wealth necessary to generate productive lives for our citizens and for government to pursue an activist agenda. In general, liberals believe that these entities representing the people have a leadership role to play in pursuing the common good.

Today's liberalism is the reverse of what defined liberal thought in the nineteenth century. At that time, liberals were opposed to the extension of the power of the state and were strongly individualistic. After all, the nation had rebelled against an intrusive and oppressive monarchy to gain its freedom. Current liberal thinking, from the 1930s onward, is not an agreed-upon recipe for government action.

Just as pizza offers a wide variety of ingredients to suit a range of tastes, so liberalism for individual liberals (like me) may have anchovies (no), three kinds of cheeses (yes), and a thick or slim crust (slim).

The basic liberal analysis starts with a perceived problem. For example, today, medical services are too expensive and do not provide adequate care for all Americans. We liberals would likely agree that any solution to this problem must involve a medical system that would include all citizens. Yet there is disagreement on how to achieve this goal.

Liberals see that the statistics on life expectancy and infant mortality show the United States is twenty-eighth in the world — a long way from number one. We understand that, in studies of the effectiveness of medical care, we fall behind Great Britain, Canada, Germany, France, Japan, and the Scandinavian nations. We liberals think something can and should be done about this, so that we no longer see headlines like the following, from the March 23, 2008, issue of the *San Francisco Chronicle*: "Gap in Life Expectancy of Rich, Poor Widens."

Similarly, liberals raise questions about the vaunted upward mobility in American society. We see the poor and some ethnic groups forming a permanent underclass, which is now being increased by those moving downward from the working and middle classes and suffering from declining opportunities in the new emerging economy.

Beyond medical care and equal opportunity, we liberals generally accept the values listed above as worthwhile goals. But we disagree among ourselves on the exact policies to achieve the desired outcomes, and we often have disputes about the breadth and depth of specific policy innovations. For example, while recognizing the necessity of intervention in the economy to lessen global warming, we disagree on how much government regulation is necessary. Similarly, liberals can support legislation deemed to be family friendly, but some of us may balk at gay marriage.

These divisions illustrate a dilemma within the liberal mind. Liberals are on an action continuum: the question may not be to act or not to act, but *how much* to act. Some seek much more leadership and involvement from a more activist government. Those wary of too much governmental control and power propose more limited approaches.

We liberals, like conservatives, find ourselves in the political middle. We are flanked on the left by progressives, socialists, and radicals of one kind or another. Conservatives have, to their right, the libertarians and religious fundamentalists. In both cases, liberal and conservative, any individual within either group may accept some beliefs of their more extreme fringes.

Some nonliberals castigate us for our seeming lack of firm conviction on issues. There is probably some truth to this, for the liberal mind is capable of seeing several sides of proposed policy solutions. Yes, we need to make American interests primary in foreign policy, but we must be aware of other nations' concerns as well.

Many liberals, and libertarians as well, reject the notion that this nation has either the right or responsibility to force its morality or political system on others. At the same time, we should operate in such a manner that our behavior models our stated values and goals.

Here again, liberals may be torn. How, we may ask, can we associate or seek accommodation with those nations whose values are antithetical to our own? The answer may well be found in a quotation from the very conservative Winston Churchill. "It is better to jaw, jaw, jaw than to war, war, war."

Clearly, Churchill did not reject the use of force in this statement, but simply stated a preference for talking over fighting. In a multipolar world, with emerging power centers and a variety of cultures growing stronger and wealthier, American liberals recognize the need for a foreign policy that takes this new diversity into account. We would say that we should respond to the reality we find ourselves in, rather than try to impose our view of what should be on others.

It is a pity that electoral campaigns do not really allow for a widespread discussion of the political philosophies that underlie our "pursuit of happiness." Perhaps some politician can do for politics in America what Barack Obama did for race relations in America. Make politics a discussable item, free of ranting and raving.

On to the Future

There comes a time in the life of those of us Americans when the policy issues we confront have projected implementation or completion dates that clearly exceed our life expectancies.

It's a funny experience to hear that some policy has a mandated date for implementation in 2024. Hell, if I live that long, I'll be ninety-three, and in all likelihood, I won't be a father to be, nor will I live to enjoy the benefits projected. Suddenly I have to confront the world beyond me; I have to recognize that my decisions and those of my peers will have their impact on the nation after we have departed.

As I scribble away on this brief essay, my wife and I are watching pundits *punditing* on the latest results in the Democratic primary race for the November 2008 presidential election. Oops, she wants to check on the score of the Giants–Rockies game. Six to three, Giants, in the ninth. Another oops. Rockies homer with someone on first, and it's now six to five. But the final out arrives on a swinging strike, ending a six-game losing streak.

Ball games have a shorter time frame — two or three hours — and at the end, there are clear winners and losers, save for the occasional tie, of course. Politics, a form of sport, has no ties; so, come November, there will be someone in the winner's circle.

That political winner will select specific proposals designed to address problems confronting the nation and, at the same time, create a record for historians to assess the success or failure of the administration. So these coming years will, in a sense, be my gift to the future. Not the contribution of a president or a senator, but nonetheless important within a democratic society.

Our children and grandchildren represent a bequest to the world beyond us. They may well choose to extend our political views for decades to come. Even as memories of us fade, there will be a residue from what we have done.

As for the immediate future, there are things to be done as we seek to make this a better nation — a nation whose famed dream needs dusting off, so that it shines once again.

More Questions than Answers

So it's McCain and Obama. Our long season of primaries has brought us to the main event.

Presidential elections are important in the USA. They set a governmental tone for at least two years, until the midterm congressional elections, and often longer. This year, we have serious issues confronting the nation and the world: Iraq, the social safety net including medical care, global warming, enormous federal and personal debt loads, and an economy sinking while the dollar withers.

None of these problems is amenable to easy solutions. Gaining the public and congressional support needed to work successfully on any one of these problems will require enormous political skill by the new president.

Overarching the specific potential crises is a rising sense that the age of American super-supremacy is waning. New powers are emerging that will challenge us economically, technologically, and militarily.

In part because of the nature of the primary process, we have little knowledge of how the two surviving supplicants for our votes will propose to resolve our national dilemmas. As the campaign moves ahead, both will set forth an agenda for the new Congress to enact.

The primary did surface some issues unrelated to actual policy making that may be determinative in the election itself. Given our national history, race may be the stickiest of these. Are we ready to elect an African American to lead us?

There was evidence aplenty, in the reporting of various state primaries, that many white Americans will not vote for Obama because he is black. There was also a lot of data — for example, from Wisconsin, Illinois, and Virginia — that he can capture white voters.

Racial attitudes became polarized around Obama's church and his black pastor's diatribe against the white power structure. Then a white guest preacher resurfaced the issue in a rant attacking Hillary Clinton. One white conservative said to me, "How can I vote for him, if that's the way they feel about us?"

White working-class voters have tended to vote conservative since the Reagan years, and Obama did not do well with this demographic group. In this coming election, if the economy does not improve, and if the Democrats come up with program ideas that have appeal to these folks, their choice may be race or economic self-interest.

McCain, too, faces a great unknown, unrelated to the specific issues confronting us. Age. At a time when fifty has become the new thirty-five, are we willing to send a seventy-one-year-old to the White House?

He is in good health, and he is a vigorous campaigner. However, stuff happens as a person ages and becomes susceptible to a whole range of physical and mental disabilities. Democrats will jump on any McCain mistake to subtly, or maybe even brazenly, question whether the mistake was age-related.

Obama has the opposite age problem. McCain charges that he is too inexperienced and naïve to handle the job. Is this equivalent to saying he's too young?

During the campaign debates, it will be fascinating to see them perform together. Who will have the energy and display a mastery of the issues? Will our perceptions be formed by the obvious age difference in front of us?

Another kind of age issue is found in the primary returns. Obama did amazingly well with young voters. They volunteered for his campaign and voted in record numbers. Historically, they have not been dependable voters; in general, they vote in numbers far below their percentage of the population. In 2004 and

2006, however, young folks showed signs of greater commitment to the electoral process and to the Democratic Party.

At the other end of the age continuum are the older women who were Hillary Clinton's biggest supporters. Will they stick with the Democratic candidate or switch to McCain in anger that their favorite didn't make it to the November play-off?

We've got to hang on for another five months as we, the people, prepare to answer the questions noted above.

In Search of Our Victory

"How many houses do you have, Dad?" asked my daughter, making a joke the day after John McCain was revealed to have seven or eight or, by one account I heard on TV, ten. The main point of the story was that he didn't know. His staff would get back to the reporter who asked the question.

Bad for the image. If you don't know how many houses you have, what else don't you know that might really be important? And, if you have a multiplicity of dwelling places, how can you relate to the millions of Americans who are having problems holding on to just one?

It's all a one-day dustup that is only tangentially related to the enormous range of issues confronting the United States and the world in 2008. We, the deciders in the presidential campaign, hear very little about the reality of our condition.

Certainly, political campaigns are about winning elections. By some quirk I'd never thought of until now, our presidential races take place in the same year as the Summer Olympics, where we see victory as golden. An odd fact: psychologists have discovered that third-place finishers — bronze — are happier about their performance than those coming second — silver. So close, and yet so far.

Watching the Olympic events, we are informed about the past records of the contestants, their current physical condition, the possible impact of the weather on any event, the training they have undertaken, etc. We know the problems they face, and they know the difficulties they must surmount to win.

If we turn our electoral process around and see ourselves as the contestants, it is clear that we, too, need to be hyperaware of what our decisions portend. One way of putting this in perspective is to ask ourselves "the Reagan question": Are we better off today than we were four or eight years ago? If we say no, we can see that we lost those elections.

The candidates claim they are running to serve our interests, yet they steadfastly refuse to explore those interests and what they propose to do about them.

Idea: After the final candidate debate, the two contestants could be given an hour of television time to introduce those whom they will name to their cabinet, along with the record these people have compiled in working with the problems they will face as cabinet members. The focus would be on proposals for future policy and the proven capacities of the selectees to get things done.

We, the deciders (sorry W), would then have a better sense of the state of the nation and the policy priorities of the two sides.

This does not preclude questioning, personal attacks of one kind or another, or commercials with vague promises of goodies yet to come. The campaign, as we have come to know campaigns, could go on to entertain the multitude.

In those final two hours, when we could see and hear the people who will be responsible for serving the interests of the American people, we can then be informed deciders.

THE JOURNEY

There is a street, a road, an avenue, or in some cases, a freeway in every city in America named Ambition. It can be short or long, wide or narrow, and for those of a political bent, it leads to power.

For those seeking power, movement toward that goal involves innumerable choices. The greatest such choice involves the price of proceeding. What, the seeker may ask, am I willing to give up as I pursue my ambition? It may be more likely, however, that the question will not be posed or put in such a way as to limit the inquiry to matters financial. Other more personal costs to traveling along Ambition Avenue would have to be factored into the decision.

"Power," Lord Acton wrote in 1887, "tends to corrupt; absolute power corrupts absolutely." Following this thought, we encounter degrees of corruption, rather like an infection spreading from a cut on a finger and moving through a weakened immune system to become life threatening. We can ignore the tiny wound, and we often do, until we begin to feel a more significant discomfort. But what if we feel no discomfort while the poison spreads throughout our bodily systems?

What if the power seeker is pure of heart with the ambition to do good for the city, state, or nation? How does he or she recognize the possible corruption abounding — while the potential corrupters around him or her focus on their self-interest and their desire to make use of the power seeker's ambition for their own ends?

Ambition can be blinding. The goal shines brightly, obscuring the dangers of the pursuit. The clamoring crowds, the approving toadies, or the powerful, looking for the ambitious to seduce or buy, line the avenue to cheer. The journey becomes, at its most extreme, an exercise in purchased adulation.

The seeker thus gathers the symbols, the artifacts, and the people, so that power is no longer the goal but the natural fruition of the ambition that has been the motivation for the journey.

Having power is one thing, and exercising it is quite another. Political power is a force that can be used for good or evil. Those who have sought it and obtained it have choices to make. Those corrupted en route can pay the price they acquiesced to during their journey.

Some will come to power motivated by a sense of the public welfare, and they must struggle with themselves and their supporters to define that elusive concept. First comes the definition, then the exercise of power to achieve the agreed-upon end.

Theodore Roosevelt described the situation in this way: "Power undirected by high purpose spells calamity; and high purpose by itself is utterly useless if the power to put it into effect is lacking."

Power is there to be used. How it will be used depends on the hearts and minds of the powerful. The price they have paid to gain their position will be inferred from the ways in which they use their power.

Commentators on our Iraq and Afghanistan adventures have been reminding the nation that we cannot win unilaterally — and that we must gain the hearts and minds of the Middle Eastern and Central Asian populations.

Since 82 percent of Americans believe the nation is headed in the wrong direction, the hearts and minds of the populace are clearly not in sync with the current administration. That leaves open for conjecture the state of the hearts and minds of the politically powerful. Will they be willing and eager to exercise their power uncorrupted by those forces that have traditionally controlled our government?

The question, then, is not related to the ambition needed to pursue political power. It is related to the capability to resist the temptations along the way and, once power is gained, the willingness to accept responsibility for specific actions. Again, Teddy Roosevelt nailed it when he observed, "I believe in power; but I believe that responsibility should go with power."

It is the unwillingness to accept responsibility for actions or inactions that has been a hallmark of Bush II's governance. He may have been corrupted through his adventures on the way to power or his eight years in office. But in the end, it makes no difference — he must be judged on what he has done to promote the welfare of the American people.

Over the years, Bush has been defined using a variety of unpleasant adjectives. In summary, they describe a man lacking curiosity but possessing certainty in the decisions he makes. He is seen as a man to whom doubt is an alien experience. Perhaps he should have read and thought about a brief quotation from Dag Hammarskjöld, United Nations Secretary General in the 1950s and 1960s:

"The longest journey / Is the journey inwards / Of him who has chosen his destiny."

O Woe Is Me

So it's three days to lever-pulling season. Or touching a screen. Or filling out the form. Whatever. November 4, 2008 — not Election Day, but the last day to elect. On TV, the pre-Election Day choice makers are shown lining up in enormous numbers in those states that allow early voting. Some news stories report on folks waiting for up to five hours to fulfill their civic responsibility.

It seems that Democrats are turning out a bit more than Republicans, and that should favor Barack Obama's candidacy. This is in line with nationwide polling results showing the Illinois senator to be up five to nine percentage points.

But — I say — it's still a race in progress. Well-paid pundits predict a potential closer race as we reach November. They, the wise ones, cite historical precedent as the basis for their prognostications. So, it is likely to get tighter in the next days.

As an Obama partisan, my fears runneth over. What if? I recall the "Bradley effect," named after L.A. Mayor Tom Bradley, an African American who lost the race for California governor despite being ahead in voter polls going into the election. And kids never turn out in big numbers. The same thing with African American voters. Folks like me, social security and Medicare recipients, we'll be there, but we tend to vote Republican.

Then there's the Palin problem. Will she be able to hold on to those enraptured folks who delighted in her *Jane Six-Packness* earlier in the campaign? The pollsters say she's lost much of her appeal. Do they know that for sure?

As partisan as I am, it's hard for me to imagine a McCain victory. The country is in an economic dumpster while Middle

Eastern quagmires soak up our resources. The incumbent Republicans have been in charge for the eight-year decline-and-fall we are now experiencing. In a fit of fairness, I must admit that the problems noted above predate 2001 and that Bill Clinton's administration contributed to our current angst.

More to furrow my ample forehead. The *McCainies* are projecting victories in Pennsylvania, Florida, and Ohio. If this becomes real — oh, my!

Hold on! Another poll analyst says that, right now, Obama can count on over 340 electoral votes. But he adds that McCain has moved up in the last few days.

The ultimate question, however, is not who will win — but what difference will it make to the future of the nation?

Here, too, I have worries. Whoever wins will have little chance of addressing the enormous problems Americans face today. A fouled-up medical care system, a decaying infrastructure, and our international debt are all too real. Obama and the Democrats might be able to do something about Iraq, but that leaves Afghanistan.

Putting all of the above aside, I remember my guys are the Democrats, and we seem to know how to lose in the late innings.

THERE'S MORE TO DO

It's over.

The Phillies won. They're the champs for 2008. Next year they come back to defend their title while wearing their championship rings.

In that other interesting contest, the winner gets no ring and has to begin the battle for another victory immediately — months before he moves into the big white house in the District.

With the Phillies, their fans will hope for another successful year. They will come to the games and cheer for the team as long as it wins. A bunch of losses will generate anger, boos, and a search for scapegoats.

Expectations will also be high for the new president. He's made a lot of policy promises, and the people who elected him want results. He is, after all, their employee. No productivity leads to disaffection and a loss of faith in the process. What's the point in being active and committed if the guy you chose can't get the job done?

The paragraphs above were written before Election Day and the overwhelming Obama triumph. It's two months-plus to January 20, and the demands for action related to the national/international economy are rising. Obama is responding by making clear what he wants from the lame-duck session of Congress, which will convene in mid-November. He has also let the world know that there is only one president in office and, until the inauguration, that is George W. Bush.

This relationship, Obama-Bush, is going to be tricky. Bush is so unpopular (28 percent approval rating) that it seems Obama could take initiatives and assume a real leadership role, and the public would cheer him on. But he knows that his role today is restricted by law and by the conventions of history.

The serious nature of our difficulties has been reflected by Obama in his victory address and at his first press conference. Something about his facial expressions, his response to the celebratory crowd, and then to the reporters suggest that the gravity of his responsibilities is now a part of his being.

In approaching his new job, he has some priorities in mind, and he is making them clear to the electorate and to the legislators in the Congress. He feels that there needs to be some immediate action to stimulate the economy. He acknowledges that fear permeates the middle class and the poor. His task is to provide hope that "Yes, we can." He was elected in part as a messenger of hope. Like FDR in 1932, he can keep hope alive by his actions and his willingness to address the issues confronting him and us.

He and his team of esteemed economists may just be guessing at what will work, and they know they will make mistakes in the months and years ahead. What they must be able to do is prevent the triumph of fear over the hope they currently symbolize. The nation, like the Philly fans, will be able to tolerate some losses; what we will not put up with is inaction and excuses. We hired him, and we have expectations for performance.

THE PAIN OF LOSING

Because I am a registered Democrat, I'm used to losing elections. From 1968 through 2004, three winners and seven losers in the presidential pony trot. This year, 2008, may portend a better record in the future. Possibly, I can put away my quadrennial grousing over the pain of yet another loss.

But until last week, I have never even begun to feel an election loss like some, maybe most, gays and lesbians in California are experiencing. The passage of Proposition 8, a constitutional ban on same-sex marriage, is for them a far more personal matter than G. H. W. Bush clobbering Michael Dukakis was to me. On one level, Prop 8 took away a court-approved right to marry the person of their choice. On a far deeper level, it struck at their humanness. Their perceptions of themselves as worthy human beings.

I was surprised at the depth of feeling I encountered in a discussion with a lesbian educator. She is in a long-term relationship, and she and her partner have two children. They are a family.

My friend's anger at what the voters had said came through in her words and in her voice. This terribly rational woman could not contain her fury and her disappointment. She singled out two of her neighbors who knew of her situation and had "Yes on 8" placards stuck into their front lawns.

"What are they feeling and saying about us? Are we some kind of vile infectious subhuman species? Are we supposed to move out of the neighborhood we've lived in for years?"

Her anger extended to the voters' impact on her two children, ages twelve and four. The youngsters are well aware that they are part of a two-mommy family and that there are many other families like their own. In the nastiest aspect of the "Yes on 8" campaign, gay and lesbian families were assailed as a form of perversion. What do the children in such families take from this kind of labeling? What kind of bullying or name-calling are they facing in school?

One of the great ironies in all this fuss and fury over the word "marriage" is its decline in the straight community. Divorces. Remarriages. Serial monogamy. They are all, if not rampant, at least popular.

The case for Proposition 8 was supported by both the Catholic and Mormon churches. Great gobs of money that could have gone to providing services for the poor among these groups of believers were flung to the *yessers*. The churches have the right to forbid their priests and pastors from performing same-sex weddings. Why not leave it at that?

The issue remains unresolved. The courts may invalidate the constitutionality of Prop 8. One post-election poll has indicated that 8 percent of voters who chose *yes* have changed their minds and would vote *no* in another election. Both the *no* and the *yes* camps are keeping their troops mobilized.

As our discussion of the election moved on, I thought about the pain suffered by the innocent victims of this divisive campaign. What difference does it make to me, or society at large, if people who are committed to one another — and want to sanctify that commitment, legally and spiritually, through a marriage ceremony — can exercise that right?

Stand by Your Man: A Play in One Act

Time: Several decades in the future
Place: Republican Valhalla
Characters: George W. Bush and Richard Cheney

Cheney: I'm glad we have this opportunity to talk. It's been too long. When was our last big talk?

Bush: Oh, about 2008. It's been a while.

Cheney: I know. It's like you've been avoiding me.

Bush: Oh, no. Just busy.

Cheney: Well, I've wanted to tell you how I've promoted and protected our legacy. There are a lot of leftists, socialists, and do-gooders still trying to tear away at our accomplishments.

Bush: Our legacy is safe.

Cheney: In good part because of my work after the pinkos won in 2008. Those guys really had it in for us, but I fought back. I could have used your help.

Bush: Getting the funding for the library took a lot of time. And then there were all the speeches.

Cheney: What I've done has to be a big part of the library. Remember, I was the one who was pushing for an all-out war on terrorism, Iraq, Afghanistan, Al-Qaeda, using advanced intelligence techniques...

Bush: Our legacy is safe. There were seven years, and there was no second attack on us.

Cheney: But there would have been if we hadn't got the intelligence right.

Bush: Those were tough times.

Cheney: Yes, they were. It required us to be tough. Those FBI guys and their namby-pamby questions were setting us up for failure. It was my lawyer Addington and I who made the case for enhanced investigation techniques. You signed off on it.

Bush: I did a lot of signing in defense of our nation.

Cheney: But where were you when they started coming after us? All that stuff about torture and waterboarding. They didn't know what they were talking about. I hear that they're still at it.

Bush: Tough times require tough guys.

Cheney: I did all I could do. You just sat in your new big house. And you didn't pardon Scooter Libby when you should have.

Bush: It was a difficult time.

Cheney: Sure was. Where was the guy who won in 2000 and 2004? Where was the guy who could make decisions, who trusted his gut responses?

Bush: We stood together.

Cheney: Yeah, but then I was all alone. You didn't seem to care. And I got my lawyer to press those ideas about the unitary presidency to make the office stronger and give you more power.

Bush: Yes, you did.

Cheney: Remember what Nixon said: "When the president does it, that means that it is not illegal." We were building you a stronger presidency that our enemies could not ignore. You could and did do what was necessary.

Bush: That was useful. I have to go now. Got a meeting of the baseball Hall of Famers who are down here. Gotta talk about the integrity of the game. Glad we had this talk. Bye.

On Governing

" Come now, and let us reason together." Lyndon Johnson used the ancient saying (originally from the Bible's Book of the Prophet Isaiah) when he wanted to twist an arm in the governmental decision-making process.

Of late, President Obama's been telling the nation that we need to lower the decibels in our political discussions and become more receptive to sweet reason. A splendid idea, but difficult to put into play because of the fractured nature of our political life.

Just two weeks ago, I was one of four reasonable people who sat down before dinner to enjoy a glass of wine and chat a bit — catch up with what was going on in our lives. One of us, I forget who, said he had been following the big health care debate and that he was getting upset.

No. This is not about health care, just as the goings on in Washington, and in town hall meetings across the nation, are not about health care.

Forthwith, an account of our reasoning together:

Irene: I just love the way the president is able to make his case for change. He just wants to work together with people.

Bradley: That's all well and good, but when's he gonna do something?

Jerome: But he is doing something. He's fulfilling his campaign promise to change the culture in Washington.

Rodney: So what's that got to do with health care? We need him to reason with senators like LBJ did. Shake 'em up.

Irene: We've got to get beyond all that old stuff. The country can't get anywhere if we keep insulting one another or try to —

Jerome: That's right. If we don't agree on civilized debate as we try to govern ourselves, it just makes divisions in the country get worse.

Bradley: Baloney (or words to that effect). You have to deal with the world as it is. He's being paid to get things done for the country. He should get on with it.

Jerome: You want a dictatorship? We need to have all voices heard and respected. Then he can provide the inspired leadership we need. He has the power to bring us together.

Rodney: Nuts. He has to understand this is a time for testing him. They're going to try and kill health care, so they can kill him politically. He's got to be tough and show he's willing to use the weapons in his political arsenal.

Irene: He's proven he's tough. He can't just give in to the old culture of division and vituperation. What's the point of that?

So on we went to the second glass of wine and beyond. Not health care but the persona of the president became our agenda. How do you be president?

For me, the issue is simple. Whoever resides at 1600 Pennsylvania Avenue got there because he or she wanted to be there. And there is the seat of power in the nation. If you chase after it and you get it and you don't use it to accomplish what you want to do, you're a fraud.

Sure, Obama can talk nice, and he doesn't have to respond in kind to scurrilous attacks from the other side. But in the end, he has to make clear to the senators and congresspeople, that he is willing to punish his adversaries and reward his friends.

This does not mean he must go through some guilt-ridden catharsis with the public. I don't know how many arms President Johnson twisted, or how many congressional districts did or did not get new highways or bridges because of his actions. He got things done — civil rights and Medicare among those things. And the irony of his time was that his fear of appearing weak kept this country fighting in Vietnam.

Like poker, you've got to know when to hold 'em and know when to fold 'em.

A Report Card on Obama

Members of the Bush II government talk about the "arc of history" as a means to slide judgments about their work down the road apiece.

They certainly don't want to address the current assessment that they participated in one of the worst administrations in our history.

It is now a year after they packed their belongings and departed the halls of governance. The new kid on the block has brought in his team. How has he done in his twelve months in office?

Any judgment here will, of course, be subjected to that afore-mentioned arc of history years from now.

Mr. Obama has encountered expectations on the part of his supporters that were way beyond his capacity to deliver, even though his party controlled both houses of the legislature. The Democrats have always been a hetero-doctrinal group, with large numbers from the liberal end of the American political spectrum and a group of far more conservative legislators.

Obama chose to make reform of the medical system his premier issue at the start of his tenure, and the Democratic Party's inability to control its members in the Senate was a bit of a problem.

In addition, while Obama's policies, working in coordination with the Federal Reserve, appear to have successfully prevented failure of the banking system, they have been more marginally effective in coping with the ten-plus percent unemployment rate.

The prevailing view is that significant improvement in the job market will be extremely slow.

Support for further federal stimulus is waning as the projected deficit has risen. Here again, the gap within the Democratic Party limits the president's freedom of action. The liberals say a more short-term deficit is not as important as getting people back to work; the conservatives look at the deficit as a rising tsunami about to engulf the nation.

Thus, Obama's effectiveness has been limited by the political realities in the legislature. Also, there are still executive branch leadership jobs unfilled. Both the legislature and administration are at fault here. This, too, hampers what the government can do.

Among voters, there seems to be a wall of anger directed at both parties and the government in general. The continuing unemployment problem and the high rate of housing foreclosures have generated a sense that while the government saved the banks, it has ignored the needs of the general public.

Obama's limited effectiveness is, in large part, due to the nightmare he inherited from the previous administration. But given that, he has fallen far short of what his supporters expected while, at the same time, generating hostility and anger among his opponents.

As a supporter, I share the disappointment expressed by his followers. However, he is in some degree a victim of a fractured governmental system. If there has been a failure to address and to solve our national problems, the blame must be apportioned broadly.

As to foreign policy, there has been some success in softening the American image around the world. Obama and his secretary of state seem to work well together, but substantive achievements in foreign policy are lacking. The issues that confronted the nation on inauguration day — China's economic policies, Iran and the bomb, Israel-Palestine, Iraq, Afghanistan, Pakistan, Russian policy with its neighbors, global warming, among others — are still there.

So today is State of the Union Day. How honest will Obama be? It seems he will focus on the economy and on cutting the deficit. This runs straight into the major economic problems — unemployment and budget crises in many of the fifty states.

Were I to give a one-year grade to the president, it would be an incomplete. He has yet to master the role of an executive leader. Perhaps Year One has been a learning time for this bright and articulate politician. Let us hope. The arc of history will tell the tale.

Who Owns What?

There's sure as hell a lot to be upset about these days. The enormous oil spill in the Gulf of Mexico; the illegal/unethical manipulations of our big financial institutions; the governmental — federal, state, and local — budget holes; immigration reform; and there are more — how about climate change?

But somehow what disturbs me most these days is the breakdown of the American political system. It's there in front of me on the TV, the radio, the newspapers and periodicals. And the Net.

Listen to the bluster and the inanities coming from D.C., from state capitols, and from our city councils. The blusterers can be either Democrats or Republicans, though it seems to my biased view that the Reps have a firm lead in the contest.

I have been an observer-participant in politics since late in the 1930s. I have traveled a long road from conversations over family dinners and holiday celebrations. Republicans were the good guys; Democrats were bad, bad, bad. My uncle, a physician, strongly argued that President Franklin D. Roosevelt suffered from syphilis, not polio. Sort of like the "birthers" today and their Obama-was-born-in-Kenya mantra.

Over time, I left the Reps but not before being president of the 19th District Young Republicans. Since then, I've been a Democrat, liberal, progressive.

I've taken part in lots of campaigns, served as president of the Pacifica Democrats and won four elections to the local school board — a nonpartisan office. I like the game, and I understand the role of politics in a democratic society.

My recent agonies began with the health care debate, where neither party put forward the facts about our current medical system. They agreed it cost too much, but there is a mountain of evidence as to its low quality relative to other industrial nations. "We have the best medical system in the world," the Republicans would say. The Democrats talked about cost, the long-term crisis in Medicare, and how much the public spends to provide care for the uninsured.

In the Senate, party loyalty became the real issue, and Republicans held tight. A fancy parliamentary procedure won the day, and a sort of reform was passed.

Wall Street reform? Both sides agreed it was needed but how much, how tough? There was bipartisanship; then there wasn't. Republican House Leader John Boehner and Senate Leader Mitch McConnell talked with Wall Street types and seemingly got their marching orders.

Something will pass, but it is not likely to be sufficient to contain the greed that created our financial crisis. And, in the end, it is the all-powerful buck that discourages me.

"Money," said Jess Unruh, a leader of the California Democrats in the sixties and seventies, "is the mother's milk of politics." But it's gone beyond milk, martinis, and warm knees. Now millions and millions of dollars in political contributions, and even more millions spent on lobbying systems to control legislative votes, create a high hurdle for those legislators who might choose to vote for the national interest rather than some watered down "compromise" favoring the powerful.

I feel a rant coming on, but I'll hold off a bit and just mention the Supreme Court decision that gave corporations all the rights of individuals to contribute to political campaigns. This decision by the activist court reversed longstanding federal policy. The search is on for legislation restoring the status quo ante (ah, a memory trace from some history course a half century ago).

Corporate America or America *Corporatized* has amassed a recent record of unmatched thievery from the public. The savings and loan scandals of the 1980s and 1990s, the Enron mess, plus the numerous screwups of the early 2000s. The current "great recession" and its unrepentant perpetrators.

Good business, like good government, like good families, is built on trust. How dumb do we have to be to trust our financial titans after three major screwups in twenty years? We are left to trust government to protect us from the evildoers.

But then we face the reality. Who owns the political process and thus the government?

Making Choices

In this confusing and increasingly dangerous world, how does one fulfill the responsibilities of the good citizen in a democratic nation?

This question disturbs me as I seek to understand and act on my understanding of just two of the weighty issues that confront Americans today. I limited myself to two because they make the case for the plethora of problems we voters face.

Problem one: global warming — how are our actions impacting what may be a natural warming cycle in temperatures around the world?

There are contradictory opinions galore floating about on our ever-expanding communication media. On one hand, the majority of scientists studying the warming phenomenon support the idea that human behavior is increasing the rapidity of change and, ultimately, the amount of increased heat we will experience in the years ahead.

They cite, among other things, melting glaciers, increasing instances of species extinction, rising salinity in oceans, changes in seasonal temperature patterns requiring alterations in planting and harvesting schedules, and on and on.

But there is, of course, a second- and probably a third- or fourth-hand argument to be looked at. There are scientists refuting the views of the majority. There are corporations concerned about sacrifices they may be asked to make to forestall the potential world disaster. Individual decision making around common issues — a car purchase, a vacation, new appliances, turning off the lights at home — can all be related to global warming.

In addition to the scientific naysayers, a sizeable crew of ideological opinion makers deny all the furor about our overheating planet. A large number of true-believer environmentalists also discount those who suggest we go slowly in dealing with earth's warming.

Within all this, how do I, the average guy trying to be a responsible person, adopt a code of belief and behavior that will be a response to what is really happening vis-à-vis our climate?

My rational self says stick with the scientific consensus. They know what's going on, and they have the evidence to support their conclusions. But, hey, some of the deniers from within the scientific community have their own data sets. And besides, the earth has gone through climate change since the big bang. Sure, the ideologues are a bit off the wall, but maybe they have a point.

Issue number two is more complex and opaque. War. We are, today, involved in two armed conflicts, one that appears to be mostly over with claims of victory, and a second about to enter a new and decisive stage.

So what do we voters think about war as we approach ballot day? Who, if anyone, should we look to for guidance and wisdom? Decisions about war are not subject to scientific inquiry before the fact. Neither of the wars we are fighting today has a clear definition of victory attached to it. Beyond this confusion are concerns about our ally Pakistan and its nuclear weapons. So do we increase the conflict in Afghanistan to limit Pakistan's Islamic militants?

Then Iran and its presumed effort to develop atomic weaponry pose perhaps a larger question. Is a preemptive strike our best chance to resolve the issue? What about the impact on the Muslim world?

Thinking about this stuff causes headaches and heartburn. Again, who do we turn to for guidance? As we, the cadre of citizen deciders, struggle through the intricacies and subtleties of defining victory and fighting wars, where do we turn for legitimate assistance?

In the past, newspapers, magazines, and TV news organizations were sources of information that we assumed was factually based. Now in the hyper-opinionated world of communication, contrasting stories and versions of truth vie for our attention and our belief. Fox and MSNBC represent contrasting worldviews and attempt to bring us to their side of the issue.

On Election Day our choices are not framed in terms of what we should do about global warming or war. Our job is to select people who will best represent our views on these and the multiple other issues our government must deal with.

We can't all sign up at the local college to do political research. Citizenship requires an informed citizenry, but becoming and remaining informed is difficult and time consuming.

While some of the issues we must deal with are quite profound, the process of information gathering and personal decision making may prove to be our greatest challenge.

Choosing a Response

Damn it! Get Angry! (Or maybe just act angry.) That's what I wanted from the president in his press conference centered on the BP oil spill. It's what I didn't get and, in thinking about it later, I was glad he was the "cool" Obama, calm under pressure.

Anger, justified many times over, can be found all over the land. The people immediately affected, the folks who want action, those who participate in the blame game, and even guys like me are angry, and we express our anger eagerly.

But anger, front and center in a public display, is not the Obama we know and elected to lead us. In a book covering the new president's ascension to power and his first year in office, Jonathan Alter compares Obama's temperament and decision making with Mr. Spock on *Star Trek*, because he chose reason and logic over emotion.

So there is a presidential decision here, be it consciously thought out or instinctive. The result is a series of press conference statements that avoid a display of anger in favor of a more detached intellectual approach.

Some of the ever-present commentators and pundits portray this presidential "detachment" as a political weakness separating the president from the public. If he's angry, let him show that anger and let his anger be reflected in his actions in this crisis.

Two personal incidents reflecting the power of cool over anger pop into my mind.

Once, as a high schooler, I was driving a young lady home in the evening, when I made a mistake and paid more attention to her than my driving.

The result was a minor accident resulting in a damaged fender on my father's car. I dreaded his response. He often displayed his temper within the family. This time it was different. There was no shouting, no swearing. Just an inquiry into what happened and the question: what did you learn?

Later as a father, I encountered a similar situation with our son. As we picked him up at the police station after the accident, he said, "Don't say anything." Despite my anger, I restrained myself.

In both cases there was no damage to the relationships involved, so the immediate problem could be handled without having to repair the damage done by verbal outbursts.

I understood the Obama message to the American people as:

We must stop the flow of oil into the gulf.

We must clean up the damage done to the shore and the gulf.

BP is responsible for this mess.

The federal government and the president himself are ultimately responsible for seeing that all the above gets done.

Accepting responsibility is fine. What counts is how the responsibilities are carried through. The president, whoever it may be, meets responsibilities of the office through the various agencies in the executive branch.

Leadership of those agencies is appointed by the president and, assuredly, will represent the president's thinking in doing the job. Many of the agencies are in place to regulate some aspect of national life: The Food and Drug Administration, Environmental Protection Agency, Securities Exchange Commission, and so on.

If the president does not believe in strong regulatory measures coming through the executive, the various agency leaders will reflect that view. Thus, the Bush administration did not press hard on the regulatory gas pedal, and regulation became more lax and more corporately friendly from 2001 through 2008.

Obama's acceptance of responsibility for the gulf oil catastrophe means his agency heads must play an aggressive leadership if he, the president, is to be successful in carrying out his responsibilities.

It also means that the agencies must behave in a fashion stylistically acceptable to the president. Angry imprecations and off-the-top policy actions do not reflect the Obama style. It would seem then that the federal response to BP and others will be measured but, at the same time, strongly reflect the president's need to respond to the national emergency.

So I don't get the satisfaction of seeing my president behave like I probably would. It's a far greater satisfaction knowing he is in charge of himself and the government's response to our crisis.

Gang Lands

At first glance, the two environments are vastly different. I shouldn't have looked a second time, but I did. First glance wrong.

I was trying to get the political commentators on MSNBC, one recent Friday evening. They were off, and the channel was showing their usual second-string stuff on crime and prisons. I watched for fifteen minutes or so and heard interviews with prisoners about staying safe while imprisoned.

"You've got to be sure, whatever you do, you've got your back covered. That means guys from your gang have to be with you, and everyone knows it."

How they would know it was generally a matter of race. So blacks stood with blacks; Latinos, even though there were two primary Latino gangs, stood for one another in a crunch; and the few whites had to be very vigilant.

So I knew that stuff. It was just a capsulized version of urban America — gangs, brutality, killings.

The next day Vice President Biden was in Baghdad meeting with the disputants attempting to create a new government in Iraq.

When the vice president departed Baghdad, there were no announcements about a breakthrough in the negotiations to form a government. We don't know what he said or heard in his private meetings with leaders of the various factions.

Maybe it's time to end the palaver. Put them in the Green Zone so they can have at one another in a controlled environment.

All the fancy talk about building democracy in the Middle East is gone now. It never did reflect the reality George W. claimed to perceive as the termination of his "crusade."

It does seem clear, at this point, that the Shia will be playing a major role in what emerges. This raises the specter of some type of Shia alliance between Iraq and its neighbor Iran.

For the majority Middle Eastern Sunni governments, this outcome will be unwelcome. Many of these nations have significant Shia populations. The possibility of subversion and efforts at regime change are not pleasant dream-inducers for these Sunni leaders.

If the dominant power groups within one of our prisons felt that they were in danger of losing control, the result could be slaughter.

There will be calls among the more hawkish Americans for continuing and even increasing the American presence. "We're almost there," they'll say. "Over 4,000 Americans have lost their lives. Their sacrifice for their country cannot be ignored."

As for the prisons and our expensive tenants, there are many, beyond the guards protecting their jobs, who are eager to build new facilities so that we can get the bad guys off the streets.

Prison gangs or political rivals in Baghdad — it's all about power.

ECONOMICS

Some columnists write that we geezers control economic policy in the U.S. of A. Maybe. It is certain, however, that our increasing numbers in the population have attracted the attention of the politicians among us. Cut social security or Medicare? Our voices will be heard. As I have grown older, read more, and suffered through numerous economic greed-induced crises, my 1960 conversion to the Democratic Party makes even more sense to me.

It's the Stupid Economy

Now the title above makes no sense. Economies are neither stupid nor bright or anything in between. Economists, that cadre of learned social scientists who study economies, can, however, be lumped into categories of perceived intelligence. A high or low placement depends upon the *lumper's* degree of agreement with the *lumpee's* pronouncements.

The strength of the U.S. economy is an important thing for Americans of any socioeconomic status. Strength is assessed by indices such as the level of employment, the rate of economic growth, increases in productivity, the percentage of people who own their own homes, and so forth. Statistics are plentiful; what they mean is open to conjecture.

For example, the U.S. economy currently seems to be exhibiting strength and vibrancy. Some economists see the growth in the gross domestic product and the rise in productivity as clear measures indicating a vigorous economy.

But poll data and the November 2006 election results indicate that the general public is less than sanguine about the state of the nation's economy as it affects their lives. There is, it seems, a disjunction between the learned and the just plain folks. For the citizenry, the numbers don't add up, and the reason is that they are looking at different data sets.

For the poor and the working/middle class, the numbers that matter are the rising costs of health care, the continuing and increasing threats to their retirements, the escalation of costs for higher education, and the stagnation of their income.

Add to this the many thousands facing ascending interest rates on their home mortgages, and you could get to that old Jimmy Carter word "malaise."

Are the fears justified? Yes, if you are among the millions immediately affected by these numbers. Yes, too, if you are looking to the future of the nation, because two-thirds of our economy is based upon consumption of goods and services by the populace. Whatever limits that consumption creates downward economic pressure.

For example, if the costs of education preclude large numbers of young people from going to college, their reduced earning power will limit their discretionary income. Similarly, a deflated retirement system will diminish the income available for the seniors who are a rapidly increasing percentage of our overall population.

When you couple these perceptions with the growing income gap, as noted by the president, you have a perfect setting for *disease*. If the multitude is correct, then at some point, the learned ones will have to join them and find a reason to ignore the performance categories they have previously utilized in judging our economy's performance.

Economics isn't called the dismal science by chance.

Time for a Change

A *nalyze This* is more than the title of a very funny film. It is also a very sad descriptor of the American way of life.

We can find one or multiple analyses of almost anything — presidential politics, the message from Osama bin Laden, the strengths of the New England Patriots, global warming, the subprime mortgage scam, and on and on. What, for example are the underlying reasons, both environmental and moral, for the resurgence of the banana slug population around my home?

For some things, let's forget the analysis and return to a form of reaction and behavior that we once found comforting and useful. Outrage. We need outrage. Donald Rumsfeld had the capacity and the willingness to spark that kind of response, but he has left the stage. George Bush remains, but he is protected by his high office and his failure. He provokes pity, not outrage.

We can, however, indulge our need for outrage by taking on the thieves in the home mortgage business, their abettors in the larger money and credit community, and the regulatory institutions that have generated a worldwide financial crisis.

It is inconceivable to me that smart guys and gals in nice suits did not know that offering no-down-payment loans on homes, or loans with interests rates that would rise dramatically in a couple of years, was a form of inducement fraud. Especially when these same respectable guys and gals then lumped these loans with others, commodified them as bonds, and sold them to institutions thrice removed from the people who had been seduced into the original loans. Now the bankruptcies grow row on row;

vacant houses become blighted neighborhoods; dreams become nightmares.

Sure, some speculated on the no-down-payment loans and hoped to benefit greatly from the ever-rising price of homes: let these folks suffer. But those families that saw a chance to live better and were told they could get a home equity loan to cover any increased costs — they did not deserve to be crushed.

A lot of money was made on this gimmick, and now we, the average folks and the non-average investment bankers who should have known better, will pay the price.

As a society, we're quick to put people in jail. Over two million of us have our room and board paid for in this fashion. It was a social earthquake when Martha Stewart did time for cheating with her stock portfolio. Big flippin' deal! Do we need vigilante justice? A return to public hanging of miscreants? No. We need a government that will do its job and protect its citizens from the thieves among us. Outrage, public indignation, and anger are, today, requisites for good citizenship.

The perpetrators will claim innocence and boast of the high scruples they adhere to in their business transactions. We are reminded by Robert Reich in his book *Super Capitalism* that "scruples like other marketable commodities can be purchased if the price is right." The bad guys won the first round; we're all losing the second; let our outrage triumph in the third.

WHY SHOULD WE PAY THE BILL?

A while back, a ten-year-old boy taking a piano lesson in Oakland was shot and paralyzed. The shooter was robbing a service station across the street and fired his gun wildly.

Innocent bystanders seem to be an increasing percentage of our population. The most dramatic incidents, like this one, involve loss of life or serious injury for people in the wrong place at the wrong time.

But there are other types of innocent bystanders. Like you and me sitting in our depreciating houses while watching the numbers on the TV. Declines in the stock markets are matched with a rising cost of living and increased unemployment.

Perhaps we're not bystanders but participants. We've experienced the real estate boom and the rising stock markets over the last several years and basked in the warmth of our increased financial well-being. "What goes up will stay up," was our profound assessment of the national economy. American optimism at work.

So maybe we innocently took part in the inflation of our wealth. In this situation, more had to be better. Our faith was constantly affirmed by government functionaries, even the almost-sainted Alan Greenspan, and the numerous economists and gurus who pervaded the media. We can proclaim our innocence in the same fashion that a fair young maiden can assert seduction, or worse, by an amorous adventurer. We just didn't know what would happen in that situation.

And, as in the case of the maiden, we closed our eyes to potential negative outcomes. Our innocence was based upon hope.

Hope, as we have learned in the last two decades, is a city in Arkansas.

We have not been innocent — foolish, perhaps, in our fantasies of ever-increasing riches. And we have not been bystanders. We have been active participants in creating the mess we are in. But beyond you and me and the rest of the middle-class and working-class Americans, there are those who knew what was going on — and who have benefitted from the economic collapse we are experiencing.

There is now a rush to confront the crisis. "Let's stimulate the economy" is the great cry, as politicians and interest groups stake out the territory that will, in the end, prove their virtue.

Good enough. But no one seems to be looking at what can be done to prevent this type of catastrophe in the future. Banks and other lending institutions — making home loans without checking the borrower's income or demanding a down payment, while promoting deals with interest rates that will literally explode upward in a few years — have behaved as predators. Their prey has been the poor, the young, and the dreamers.

We know what has occurred, including the worldwide financial problems generated through our largely unregulated home loan industry. Those who created and executed the scam need to come forward. Confession, we are told, is good for the soul. Let's hear some confessions and fortify some souls.

Sure, some of the big-shot CEOs have walked the plank. That short walk ended as they dived into a lovely severance package. We need to know more about how the home loan fantasy spread like cancer throughout the banking and lending system. How about a congressional hearing?

Congressman: What was the basis for those no-down-payment loans?

Banker: Home prices rise, so if an owner has money problems down the line, they can take out a home equity loan based on the newer, higher value of their home.

Congressman: But if home prices don't rise, and the new homeowners need cash, what do they do?

Banker: We didn't think that could happen on a long-term basis. We have a vital, strong economy and, in the end, that will carry us through any problems.

Congressman: What about those interest-only and adjustable-rate mortgages? No problem there either?

Banker: It is our considered opinion that the vast majority of these loans were good for our customers and, of course, good for those who made the loans.

Congressman: You know that there are periodic downturns in the real estate market.

Banker: Certainly. But there is usually a quick turnaround. Our economy is strong.

Congressman: There is rising unemployment. Increasing inflation. Diminishing consumer spending. Credit card delinquencies are rising. There are more and more bankruptcies and home foreclosures. You sound a bit too optimistic.

Banker: But that's our business — making the American dream a reality for as many of our citizens as possible.

Congressman: Yes, of course. And your CEO was ousted last week. What was his severance package?

Banker: It was in line with other corporations' severance arrangements.

Congressman: Oh, and that was?

Banker: Well, fifty million in cash over five years. Lifetime medical coverage. Periodic use of the company plane. And lifetime dues at his country club.

Congressman: Not bad for someone fired from a job.

Ah, failure — it has its rewards. And we, you and I, and all the working- and middle-class folks are paying those rewards. Maybe this is the punishment we must endure for being complicit bystanders.

THE WEALTH OF A NATION

There it was, right there in front of me. Jane Bryant Quinn, the *Newsweek* finance writer, said it. And millions of us heard it.

"We have to understand, the United States is becoming a poorer nation." But how can that be? We're number one! We're the richest, most powerful nation in history. The American economy is the envy of the world; the living standards of the American people are unrivaled. All you need to do is look around you. It's all there.

Yes, it is. And you and I can see it and feel it.

- Home values are declining and will continue to decline for a while.
- Our 401(k)s are dropping as the stock market declines.
- Neighborhoods look decrepit as the number of homes in foreclosure rises.
- School districts are preparing to lay off teachers.
- Unemployment is rising.
- The dollar is in free fall.
- Inflation pressure is growing.
- Credit card accounts are collapsing.

Perhaps most telling of all: The president says we're going through a difficult time (but of course the strength of the economy will carry us through).

Right. "Mission accomplished."

It is one thing to identify and explore the symptoms of a disease or a social problem and quite something else to be able to prescribe an effective remedy or policy. I will make no pretense of knowing what to do. I shall simply explore a bit of the fantasy that got us where we are.

It should be noted that fantasy is the prime determinant in Bush world policy making. Iraq stands as example #1. Weapons of mass destruction? None to be found. Democracy in Iraq? Sure, after the religious and ethnic divisions disappear in a blaze of reconciliation. Al-Qaeda's connection to Saddam Hussein? Didn't exist.

Example #2: Katrina. "Heckuva job, Brownie."

Free marketers have dominated Washington economic policy for the last forty years (the Carter and Clinton administrations advocated this view to a lesser degree than the Republican government in the 1968–2008 timeframe). So, can they provide successful policy response to our economic meltdown?

It is doubtful. As commentators and real economists use the "R word" (recession) more and more, some hear, within the ongoing discussions, allusions to the "D word" (depression).

Some economists, Robert Reich and Paul Krugman for example, point to the active deregulation of business and the inactive enforcement of what regulations still exist as key contributing factors in the 2007–2008 economic mess.

Within the administration, those who will be making the big decisions keep telling us about the "underlying strength" of the American economy. But they are not very specific about what those strengths are — and how they will function to bring us out of the doldrums. They do not address the relative decline in the middle class and the widespread belief that our society is becoming more unfair.

If Quinn is correct in her assertion that we are becoming a poorer nation, the unfairness must be magnified in the future. The wealthy, very wealthy, and super rich will be able to, through their financial and political power, ensure that their portion of the diminishing wealth will continue to grow.

This kind of economic stratification does not portend good tidings for American democracy. It is the middle class, and those with hopes to rise to that level, who form the foundation for an open and vibrant political life.

The 2008 election and its aftermath may prove to be a pivotal predictor of the future of American democracy. If current economic trends continue, the populace will demand more active government intervention. Employment programs, greater regulation, tougher enforcement of immigration, maybe even protectionism will all be on the table. And, oh yes, higher taxes on the wealthy.

"May you live in exciting times" is an old Chinese curse. How much excitement can we stand?

Get an Education

Damn, they're smart!

First they phony up a bunch of fancy mortgage deals — no down payment, no income requirements, no interest payments for two years, etc. Then they bundle these risky deals and sell them around the world.

Commissions beget commissions and so on. Big bucks abound for the creative financiers.

Boom into bust. Foreclosures become routine. Bankruptcies follow. Home values plummet. People who believed in the American dream, which had been assiduously peddled to them, are now caught in a nightmare.

Again, the movers and the financial shakers exhibit their innovative spirit. Quickly, the columnists, economists, and politicians begin to blame the victims for the crimes that have been committed against them.

This is not to ignore the foolishness and ignorance of those families that took advantage of all those opportunities that were too good to be true. A seeming good deal unleashes the latent greed in most of us. For those who had been struggling to survive, it must have seemed like Santa had arrived.

There is irony in this. The McCain campaign touted the underlying strength of the American economy because our workers are creative, hardworking, and productive. "You are our strength, but please leave the keys with the collections people."

The story line now is: it's their fault because they fell prey to the fantasies paraded before them. So we have hookers on the street corners supporting their pimps, and we spend our time arresting the Johns.

It's an uneven battle; the *Yalies, Stanfoos,* and *Harvards* have the connections and the resources to parade their innocence — "We were victimized by all those people we helped to buy a home."

But we have discovered that those smart guys were too smart by half. They have created a worldwide financial crisis that has already destroyed many once-respectable firms and threatens to unravel the house of cards labeled "the international financial system."

It appears to be a stretch to make Joe Six-Pack and his relatives the bad guys in the continuing drama. There are courses in ethics in those hotshot universities across the nation that have spawned the CEOs, COOs, and CFOs who are seeking absolution while banking those enormous checks they got on their way out the door.

Justice is an abstraction. Like an abstract painting, it can be hard to define. What is clear in our present dilemma is that working-class Americans have been diddled by the movers and shakers and that, therefore, we're all shaking in our boots.

A WRATHFUL WINDBAG

In the end, it was just another almost. Lots of them in life.

Our financial advisor, a genius up to September 15, 2008, called a couple of days ago and wanted to know if I would appear on a TV news show to comment on our current economic disaster. My specific role would have been to express my views as a retiree and an older investor.

But I was off playing old folks doubles, and by the time I returned home, my chance at TV fame had disappeared. Another loss for the vast television public.

As my vision of fame and riches dissipated, I poured myself a glass of cheap white wine and began to formulate what I would have said, if I had had the chance to say it.

My first remarks would have expressed the anger that I feel. Several people I've spoken with about the meltdown echoed my sentiments. We're losing our savings every day, and the "masters of the universe" who got us into this mess sit comfortably with their immoral gains from the subprime mortgage scam. Then there is the other gang, the fired executive officers who led their enterprises into failure while they walked away with millions in golden handshakes.

Do they take responsibility for what they have done? Hell, no! Well, if they aren't responsible, who is? They jump to the dais to identify the sinners — it's those people who took out mortgages they couldn't afford.

Which brings us to another gaggle of culprits, the folks who sold the mortgages knowing, but not telling, that in many instances the costs of the mortgage would rise and could be met only through borrowing on the equity in the house. There would be sufficient equity only if the value of the properties kept on rising. The courts will be hearing fraud cases for a good bit of time.

Somewhere in this crocodile-infested swamp are the skillful technicians who created new financial instruments in the 1990s, which the investment bank people had a hard time understanding. These guys and gals are cousins to the people who began to bundle the mortgages into bonds and then sold them around the world.

While I, and many millions of our citizens, look at the monthly statements depicting our current financial status and shudder, the privileged class noted above makes plans for their next voyage on the Mediterranean.

I'm still not through with anger. Some of our employees, those folks we regularly hire and rehire and occasionally fire, who are supposedly our government leaders, have earned our wrath.

My rant here begins at the top, with President George W. Bush. The worst president in the nation's history. The man who set the tone and provided the model for his administration. His ideology, inattention to detail, and lack of introspection have betrayed us and made our lives more uncertain and dangerous.

It is important to acknowledge that we, the people, have been at fault too. We chose a man and a party to govern us who seem to believe only in less government and low taxes. For them, government is a giant whirlwind incapable of doing anything other than sucking dollars out of our pockets. Under their control, the government has gone on to validate their beliefs.

Then the financial crisis hits, and to whom do the antigovernment types turn? The only institution standing, their *bête noire*, the federal government will bail out the nation. Irony upon irony.

Anger is not enough. My audience has probably heard much of this before. What can we find beyond wrath?

How about punishment for the guilty? The good people of the United States are being severely punished as a result of the actions and inactions of the actors identified earlier. Oops, more anger.

We are told now by those who deregulated our economy that we need new regulations. Good. Let's rebuild the structure with severe penalties for those who would break or bend the new rules.

Is there any hope beyond the creation of new — or revival of old — regulatory authority? No and yes.

No. The hole we are in is too deep, too profound for fixes — private, national, or international. There is little, maybe nothing Obama or McCain can do that will point the way to the unification of a very divided nation and to a politically sustainable program of reform and rehabilitation.

At some point, the new government will have to cope with the reality that we are no longer *"Numbah One."* Nations and peoples no longer trust us, given our failed adventure in Iraq and our subprime mortgage policy that generated the global financial crisis.

Add another ton of irony to our current dilemma. Too much borrowing — public and private — put us into this mess, and now we are providing public funds to private banks to stimulate lending.

Yes. "This nation will survive and it will prosper," said Franklin Roosevelt seventy-five years ago, facing the Herculean task of inspiring a population in despair.

The near future, the next five to ten years, will hurt. We will have to alter our way of life to take account of straitened circumstances. Economic policy will have to focus on job creation that is centered on rebuilding our infrastructure, along with establishment of new energy sources. We may even have to put aside some of our narcissistic and wasteful technological toys.

In the end, it may be our technological skill reservoir that will lead us out of this morass. But we will have to strengthen our kindergarten to Ph.D. educational system so that we become a learning society and continue to attract foreign students to our graduate schools.

To achieve the above will require leadership of the highest order. Washington, Lincoln, and Roosevelt answered that need in their eras. Is there someone ready to take on the leadership role that they modeled?

Those folks who didn't get to hear me in my TV debut are lucky. What a windbag I turned out to be!

GUTS AND GUILT

It must have taken a lot of guts to testify in front of the world that your personal ideology, a set of ideas that had driven your decisions for decades, was faulty.

So it was with admiration that I listened to the once-revered Alan Greenspan testify before a congressional committee recently. He owned up to the role his beliefs played in his decision making as chairman of the Federal Reserve. He said he was "shocked" by the behavior of bank executives who ignored the best interests of their stockholders as they took care of themselves.

In part, my admiration reflected the fact that one of our employees had taken responsibility for his actions and the outcomes associated with them. A model for Rumsfeld, Wolfowitz, Rice, Cheney, et al. And, oh yes, Bush himself. But we'll have a long wait on that one.

Governing is difficult business. To do it requires the ability and willingness to see the world as it is, make difficult decisions, and generate institutional and public support for your actions. When, as with Greenspan and those within Bush's administration, reality is obscured by preexisting visions of what reality should be, good governance is impossible.

With the emergence of the twenty-four-hour news cycle, cable television, the Internet with its varied sources (some peddling nonsense) — and the decline in newspaper and magazine coverage — openness and honesty are even more important for government. We, the people, need accurate information as we make judgments about possible government policies and go on to cast our votes.

Perhaps governmental candidness is impossible. The primary objective of elected leaders — school board members to presidents — is reelection (or so the cynics say). No president wants the public viewing his or her actions in a negative light. Thus the invention of the spin machine, which manufactures often-fanciful interpretations of what is going on.

Greenspan underestimated the power of greed to erode the foundation of the elaborate structure that he was hired to protect. The insidious greed virus infected the culture as we rushed to get ours. The old British saying, "Screw you, Jack, I've got mine," resonated through our financial lives. Now with the economy in turmoil, holding on to what we have has assumed greater saliency for Americans. The market is down, home values are down, unemployment is up, foreclosures are rising, and fear is permeating the socioeconomic atmosphere. There are projections of a deep recession, and some economic commentators have used the "D-word."

It's time for honesty from the administration and the two presidential aspirants. Rumors and fantasies have led to panic. The truth may not make us free, but it will allow us to assess our current situation as we confront the decisions that will shape our futures.

Greenspan's admission of years of ideological blindness should provide a model for others who have been close to the economic decision-making process that has gotten us to where we are. "Trickle down" and "trust the markets" become a license to steal. Similarly, the fantasists who sent us into Iraq need to fess up. Their dreams of using military force to create Middle Eastern democracy have only enhanced Iranian power in the region.

Maybe, just maybe (and don't hold your breath), Greenspan will free others to come forward with their own *mea culpas*.

How about that — a mass confession in D.C.

But who will provide forgiveness?

Damned If We Do

The good news: the American public has begun putting aside dollars again, sending the savings rate up to 3.1 percent in the last quarter of 2008, from a previous zero percent. The bad news: since Americans are not spending as they used to, economic recovery is not happening.

What are we Americans supposed to do? Economists have decried our failure to save and the consequent difficulties of banks to acquire the capital they need to lend to investors, businesses and prospective homebuyers.

Businesses need customers. Seventy percent of economic activity in the United States comes from consumer spending. Bankers need depositors. And there are lots of folk who can neither spend nor save, because they are out of work.

Thus, the cry arises across the land: "Somebody — anybody — do something!"

The answering cry comes from the newly installed national administration: "We'll do whatever it takes. Trust us."

Thirty years ago, President Reagan defined government as the problem, not the solution. Now, with a problem bigger than all outdoors, we have again accepted the idea that government could actually be effective as a problem solver.

Ironically, it took the incompetent and problem-creating administration of the antigovernment George W. Bush to bring us to the point where government has become our hope for the future.

The 2008 election indicated that the economy was the principal political issue driving the Obama victory. News reports continue to highlight the loss of jobs, the failures of businesses, and the mortgage mess. All the news media headline the bad news, and the public wants action.

Anger and fear are the dominant emotions within the nation. Our security concerns have shifted from Al-Qaeda and Muslim fundamentalism to our economic security.

One group of folks who have been hit the hardest by the financial flameout is those who are within sight of retirement or who have just retired. The 401(k) retirement programs have suffered enormous losses, and older workers now have to think about continuing in the workforce to rebuild their nest eggs. That is, if they can keep their jobs.

(Just think how much worse all of this would have been if Bush's plan to privatize a portion of the social security program had been enacted!)

As we, the citizens, watch what is going on in D.C., we have no way of knowing if anyone there knows what to do in the face of the cataclysm. Some commentators and economists exhort us to look to 1933 and the New Deal. Others say we need to go slow, and our biggest difficulties may lie in the enormous budget deficits we are creating. A few say we should just wait it out, and the economy will adjust itself in due course.

Something will get done. And it will be big. Maybe not big enough, in which case something more will get done.

Maybe, to reprise an old punch line, we should "close our eyes and think of England." Probably not a good idea — their economy is in the dumpster right next to ours.

Recession — One Impact

He's tall, about six feet, and slender. His handshake is strong. He looks like, and he is, an outdoors person.

Jerry was in our living room because I was hiring him to do some work removing pampas grass and Scotch broom, plus some trimming of large bushes and camellias. We talked a bit about the job as he drank a San Miguel Dark.

The conversation moved on to "How's business?" The answer did not support Ben Bernanke's view that the economy is on the road to recovery.

Jerry's principal source of income is cutting down big trees. He's been doing it for twenty years and has just endured the worst slash in his income in that time.

"I used to get calls all the time. My clients would refer other people and would call me for more work. The last two months have been terrible. My income is down to about 10 percent of what it used to be. Now I'm on the phone calling people I've worked for, and there's next to nothing there."

This was not surprising. From spending everything they have and borrowing more, Americans are now saving about 5 percent of their income. That is, those who have work-related income. The unemployment rate is rising toward double digits.

I've seen innumerable TV interviews with out-of-work folks and the long lines of the jobless with resumes in hand outside some company's announced effort to hire five new sales people.

Daily, I also see stores that have closed because there are too few customers.

Watching Jerry sipping his beer brought the despair of unemployment home to me in a real way. I have only experienced one very short time without work since 1955. Even in retirement, there is a small job at a local college that keeps me productive.

Education, as a profession, has been largely immune to our economic swings. For a public school teacher and administrator, tenure and a growing population equaled job security. Consulting, plus college teaching and management, also provided more security than most jobs. Being of the left persuasion in my political reactions, I automatically have had sympathy for those who have undergone occasional episodes of unemployment.

I remember the period of unemployment my brother once experienced and how it affected the way he felt about himself during that time. It took a while for him to put himself together.

Today, with almost 10 percent unemployment and the continuing high level of home foreclosures, the erosion of self-confidence and self-respect must be approaching Grand Canyon dimensions throughout the nation.

Many economists and other assorted experts are predicting a rising employment rate in 2011. The biggest problem left by the recession may be the damage done to the American psyche. When we finally get our incomes back, we will be able to afford the psychiatrists we need today.

They're All Sorry

"I did it. I'm sorry I did it. I won't do it again. I apologize for my behavior."

We've all done it at one time or another and most of us have owned up to the *it* and apologized for what we did. But of late, the public apologies have been big shots, leaders in their professional fields. We, who have observed the actions giving rise to the apologists, are free to reject the penitents' words — or accept them and grant the forgiveness implicitly sought through the process of apologizing.

The three most prominent recent penitents — General Stanley McChrystal, the commander of the anti-insurgency forces in Afghanistan; Akio Toyoda, the head of Japan's Toyota automobile company; and Tiger Woods, the world's greatest golfer and the biggest single cause for golf's TV popularity and huge purses.

McChrystal has had at least two major episodes of apologizing to the Afghan people for civilian deaths caused by his troops. His words have been translated into Pashto, and he has been featured on Afghan television in his act of contrition. He is doing everything in his power to see "it doesn't happen again."

Toyoda and James Lentz, the firm's leader in the United States, are busy trying to save the company through accepting blame for what has gone wrong with its autos.

Woods accepted blame for his serial sexual exploits on national TV, while refusing to answer questions. This apology, dealing with his personal life, is different from McChrystal's and Toyoda's, which concerned far more serious matters.

The ranks of apologizers are still too thin. There are others who should be asking for our forgiveness for their actions and inactions. Where are you, Christopher Cox, former chairman of the Securities and Exchange Commission? If he chose to enter the apologia arena, he might say:

"I was appointed to my position by a president who had faith in the ability of markets to regulate themselves. I shared this belief, and so my agency was not as diligent in its regulatory duties as it should have been. I'm sorry that our inaction as a regulatory body helped bring on the financial crisis of 2007–2008. I was wrong."

There is a precedent for Cox coming forth. Alan Greenspan, former chair of the Federal Reserve, owned up to his errors vis-à-vis the self-regulating power of the markets.

Then there is the gaggle of executives from Wall Street firms who pushed us down the road toward doom. How about the folks running AIG, the enormous insurance operation that we, the taxpayers, have bailed out with over $180 billion? It is clear that AIG's operatives, earning enormous bonuses, had played key roles in the failure of their company and, therefore, in the national and European financial disaster. Step forward, gentlemen, and accept the responsibility for what you have done.

Still more — those mysterious quants, physicists, and mathematicians working for Wall Street, who created the new and very seductive securities that were at the heart of the boom that led to the bust of 2007–2008.

The list could go on. One thread that ties the non-apologizers together is that not one of them has been hauled into court. Maybe they didn't break any laws, and we can't give in to public anger as a form of justice, but somehow we need to know that there is accountability for those who act in an irresponsible manner and damage the nation and its citizens.

Perhaps we could have a Truth Commission, like those created in Rwanda and South Africa, in which guilt could be expiated, and the nation could move on. Somehow this doesn't seem appropriate. How about putting them in stocks (no pun intended) on Wall Street so their successors could learn from them?

A SLICE OF REAL REALITY

We live sort of alone on a hillside in a middle-class community, miles away from the nightmares of life in the inner city.

While we are isolated from the vicissitudes seemingly inherent in modern American life, we know of them and observe them secondhand through the variety of media that populate our lives. Yes, we feel the pain.

I was on my next-to-last Christmas shopping stop when I met reality. Outside the back door of this particular Borders bookstore, there was a ramp leading down to the sidewalk. Coming out the door, I turned left and looked down the ramp. A woman was just beginning to come up. I started to hurry, and she, in response to viewing my cane, urged me to "slow down."

"Thank you," I replied. As we passed at the bottom, I added a "Merry Christmas" to my thanks for her kindness. "So you've got the day off to shop," I said.

"No, I'm retired."

She looked a bit young for retirement, but I went on with, "I am too, and I hope you're enjoying it like I am."

"Well, no, not really. I was fired, and if I didn't take early retirement, I would lose my benefits."

She went on to explain more about her situation. "I'm fifty-four years old, and I worked for UCSF [the University of California, San Francisco] for twenty-three years. So now I live on $1,200 a month. I do take care of my father who is ill, so I'm not totally alone."

So there she is — one of the millions of unemployed and underemployed people in the United States. She's not a statistic, or a picture in the paper or on TV. This is a real live person whose life has been smashed in our "great recession."

Obviously, this is in no way one of the numerous "worst-case scenarios" in our economic distress. She's not an uneducated single mother or father bereft of everything in an intimidating world. She will not become a street person — homeless, ill, and hopeless. But she is a victim.

When I was a child during the 1930s depression, my father went broke. We had a loan from something called "Household Finance." We moved three times in two years as he struggled to bring home the money we needed.

This was the closest I have ever come to real poverty. With the advent of World War II, our situation improved dramatically.

So, in a way, I was a real stranger to this woman's new world. But she had one strength that I don't think I could have mustered when confronted with her problems.

"Somehow I know," she said, "God will take care of me. There is some kind of purpose here that I do not understand. I'll be OK."

Nonreligious as I am, if I called on the almighty for help, it would be in the nature of a plea, not a statement of faith.

Christmas Eve 2010, my family will gather for a festive dinner complete with packages to take home for opening in the morning. But somehow the true spirit of the season can be found in that stranger I met while I was winding up my shopping.

As we parted, I said again, "Merry Christmas."

"The same to you" she said. "And God bless you."

EDUCATION

Since age twenty-three, I have been an educator. I have been a middle school teacher, a high school teacher, a counselor, an administrator, a college instructor, a program director, a supervisor, and a consultant. All this, plus seventeen years on a school board. Lots of experience there. Today, we are risking the nation's future with our destruction of the K–12 education system — and compounding this with our failing approaches to our once-magnificent college and university system. Geezers can rant.

THE NEW KIDS ON THE NEW BLOCK

Having said it, I sat back and gazed at the group, knowing they didn't believe what I had proclaimed: "We had it tough just like you do." Just the mutterings of an antiquated, bald white guy.

And they were right. These neophyte school administrators in the class I was teaching did face more and greater problems in their professional lives than I could have dreamed of when I sat where they are now sitting.

Sure, my *compadres* and I had been forced to cope with the emerging drug problems of the sixties and seventies. Then there were the increasing tensions generated by the civil rights revolution. More hidden, there was a teen pregnancy issue. It was then that the teacher organization (read union) began to talk about strikes and actually hit the bricks occasionally. We heard a hint of something about technology, exemplified by the new copier in the office. There were demands that parents be more involved in school decision making. The list goes on, including those students smoking in bathrooms and the really screwed up kids who didn't bring their pencils to class or even (horrors!) cut classes.

We handled it all — one way or another. We were diligent and dedicated. Our schools functioned, and most of our clients graduated. Why can't the whippersnappers understand that we, their predecessors, had really had it tough?

Frankly, they shouldn't give a damn about our travails. Their issues, and the social complexities giving rise to them, make me reach for the aspirin jar — or maybe another post-dinner glass of wine.

Whereas we were largely free of state and federal pressures, except for annual evaluations of Title One federal projects, our successors have to cope with mandates of No Child Left Behind, which, if not met, can cost administrators their jobs. Encompassed within the concerns of NCLB are the multiconundrums associated with race and social class in the U.S. of A. Moving on, there are gang and violence issues that have moved beyond the inner city to suburbia. Then we have the questions surrounding family life. And. And. And.

Perhaps the greatest, and the most concealed, problem for school people today is the generalized decline in public trust of our institutions. Some of this has arisen from the "question authority" mantra of the hippie era. "Just because you're wearing a white coat and your identification tag says M.D., it doesn't mean you know more about medicine than what I get from surfing the Net."

However, the actions of our government, at all levels, have had the greatest impact on our level of institutional trust. Sure, in the "old days" there were those who challenged governmental performance and the assertions about its effectiveness, but they were a minority. They weren't subject to the daily misstatements from press secretaries and PR types spreading governmental truth.

When only 40 percent of the populace trusts the president, why should school folks do better? Educators are continually forced to prove themselves worthy of the trust of their communities.

Will these very willing and capable young people, now immersed in the continuous earthquake called school administration, be able to make our most important and local government systems work?

I don't know. No one does. But they seem eager to take on the task. So, as I sip that glass of wine, I smile and offer a toast to them and to their success.

CODE RED

It was a president who famously and futilely asked about the meaning of "is."

It was a high school principal who, in parallel fashion, explored with me the meaning of "red."

There have been times in our history when "red" had an important sociopolitical referent. There were the "reds" rousted by Attorney General Palmer in 1919 and 1920. The Russian Revolution inspired the fear behind the aggressive pursuit of communists and other leftists.

In the late forties and into the midfifties, Wisconsin Senator Joseph McCarthy led a crusade designed to identify "reds" in American government.

But this digresses from my discussion with the principal. She is an extremely competent leader of a small high school in San Francisco. Her school has a dress code, and part of that dress code bans the wearing of anything red. In this situation, students had been harassed by Latino gang members for displaying red in their clothing on public transportation. (I don't know why blue wasn't also prohibited, since this was the color embraced by the harassing gang members.)

Students wearing red, or a color that could be interpreted as red, were to be sent to the principal's office, where the following conversation would take place:

Principal: You know you're not supposed to wear red.
Student: This isn't red.
Principal: It's red. What is it, if it isn't red?

Student: It's a kind of orange.
Principal: No, it's red, and you have to go home.
Student: It is not red.
Principal: Do I have to call your parents?
Student: This isn't fair.

And on and on. It's not like the principal has nothing to do. She's trying to put together a recruiting drive for her charter school. She has two department meetings to attend. Her Board of Directors is meeting at five p.m., and she has a report on curriculum to give them. There is also the conference with a group of parents. And there are some students who wish to speak with her.

Nowhere in her training had she, or any other principal, learned how to define or identify red.

"What did you do at school today?" her husband might ask that evening.

"Oh, we had a wonderful discussion about what 'red' is," could be her reply.

And he would look at her perplexed and she would sigh and get on with the work she had brought home from school.

But Do We Need to Know?

"You can learn something new every day" is one of those old-fashioned sayings full of truth. Last Wednesday I learned something new.

Archimedes calculated with actual infinity.

So I asked a professor of mathematics about actual infinity. What is it? What sets it apart from the other infinity(ies)? He said he'd look it up — he couldn't quite remember.

Archimedes lived through most of the third century B.C. Some regard him as the greatest scientist of all time. Myth has him shouting "Eureka" after stepping into a bath and discovering a principle defining buoyancy.

I am less than buoyant in a river of my own ignorance. Archimedes was a Greek. Greeks are OK, but they think big thoughts. Maybe they even invented science.

The last science class I took was eleventh-grade chemistry. All I remember, after more than sixty years, is that Mr. Nill, the instructor, was a really good dresser. Three-piece suits and beautiful tweed jackets set him apart.

That chemistry class enabled me to meet the requirements for admission to the University of California, Berkeley. All the degrees and all the years in college classrooms have not equipped me to understand what science hath wrought and the scientific issues that confront the twenty-first-century citizen and voter.

Unfortunately, I am not alone. Recent magazine articles have pointed out our scientific ignorance and the potential problems this may cause the nation in striving to maintain its scientific and technological lead in the world.

American students are not majoring in math or science at our universities. The big payoff in finance-related fields seems to be capturing a higher percentage of our best and brightest. At the same time, foreign universities are now enrolling more students who used to cross the ocean to take advantage of our undergraduate and graduate schools.

The American economy is based upon scientific advancements. New industries have been created in the United States and spread throughout the world. Many of the graduate students from Asia and Europe who came here to study have remained here, as did the refugees from Nazi Germany in the 1930s. We have benefited enormously from both sets of immigrants.

Perhaps we Americans just don't want to work all that hard to master mathematics or science (guilty here). So the nation must import brains, as well as automobiles.

But beyond laziness, there appears to be an anti-science zeitgeist that is afflicting the nation. The current administration has been caught, on numerous occasions, putting aside science on important issues — particularly those related to the environment — to achieve some political or ideological advantage.

This attitude has even filtered down to some colleges where books on science have been banned. In one case, a small evangelical school prohibited instructors from using a text by one of the faculty that tried to reconcile Darwin and the school's theology. But then most Americans reject evolution and seem to believe the world began 4,000 years ago.

All of this would be meaningless except that, all across the land, people are being asked to vote on matters that are science-based, like stem cell research and approaches to global warming.

My ignorance, based upon my unwillingness to challenge my perceived intellectual weakness, has not served me well. Multiplied by millions, it raises questions about democracy and ignorance, as well as our ability to remain as *"Numbah One"* in an increasingly scientific and technological world.

THE EXPECTATION BLINDERS

It's a major American film in the 2007 season. The featured stars are Denzel Washington and Russell Crowe, both Oscar winners. *American Gangster* lays out two parallel stories and brings them together in the final twenty minutes.

Washington's character, Frank Lucas, is a major drug dealer in Harlem who has created an international organization importing heroin into the United States during the Vietnam War. As a result, he's worth several hundred million dollars.

It's a good flick — engaging, tense, with outstanding performances. In the course of the story, there occurs one of those scenes that probably say more than the authors intended. In this scene, a federal investigator confronts Crowe, a New Jersey police officer, in an effort to define the drug-selling organization as a product of the Mafia.

With apologies to the writer, my memory of the dialogue produces an exchange like this:

Crowe: This organization is run by and was created by Frank Lucas.

Fed: You're crazy. No nigger could create something this complex.

The film takes place in 1978. Its ramifications are evident throughout life today in the USA. "They," African Americans, suffer, as they have throughout our history, from the low expectations of the general society that have, in many instances, been internalized by individuals, families, and communities. When African American families encounter the variety of social agencies, including public school systems that are supposed to serve their needs, many often suffer through the same old low-expectation syndrome.

According to stories coming out of a recent statewide conference designed to address the achievement gap in our schools, a major contribution to that gap is the low expectations school folks have for academic competency in African American and Latino students.

As a longtime educator, I have been aware of the expectation gap for decades. And for decades, there have been workshops, courses, and community meetings designed to alter educators' approach to these students.

However, expectations in any relationship are a two-way thing. Many African American parents and kids expect the schools to fail them, and the schools proceed to do just that, thereby fulfilling expectations of failure.

Recent family-income data suggest that black family income is falling further behind that of white families. The data further indicate that the next generation of African American families will be even worse off, relative to white ones.

We are at a point where many African Americans have given up on integrated schools and are opting for all–African American educational institutions. Housing patterns are, in any event, leading in that direction.

The low expectation syndrome is also a part of the Latino school experience and that, too, goes back a long way.

So what do we do about the expectation gap? I don't know. What I do know is that simply telling people how to behave will not be effective. Somehow we must, all of us, educators and communities, work together closely, so that we come to know and trust one another on a new level.

THE DREAM CAN SURVIVE IF...

The key to American progress, 'tis said, is education — particularly a university education. That's what my folks thought and taught me and my brother back in the long, long ago.

They weren't the only ones who thought that way. It was federal and state policy. The GI Bill guaranteed financial support for veterans of World War II as they pursued higher education. For Californians, there were free community colleges, and the fees for attending the University of California were $35 a semester in spring 1949. And that huge sum also entitled students to medical care at Cowell Hospital, psychological services, and copies of the five-day-a-week *Daily Californian*, the top newspaper in the East Bay.

(In the interest of transparency, I worked there as a sports writer and editor for several years. More, but different transparency: I would not even be considered for admission today, because I would not have taken sufficient mathematics courses in high school. Not that I could afford the $7,000-plus annual tuition without loans and scholarships.)

Another barrier for prospective students is the state's financial problems. If the budget cuts proposed by the governor are adopted, over 7,000 applicants will be turned away this year.

I'm sorry, but that is not the way it ought to be. When I was growing up, California was a vibrant, forward-looking state that offered a top-notch education system from kindergarten through graduate school. We built a splendid highway infrastructure and a water system that served our biggest industry, agriculture, and a growing population.

163

We were number one. And now? Our K–12 schools rank forty-sixth in the nation in per-pupil spending. Take a ride on our freeways, highways, and roads and count the bumps, potholes, and traffic jams you encounter. Water rationing is a real possibility with our current drought (one or two storms do not end a drought), not to mention global warming.

It all takes money, and that takes leadership to raise the public willingness to invest in the future.

Where does the current state government propose to generate financial support?

Naturally it's the easy way — increase gambling revenues from Indian casinos. Let's gamble on the gamblers to pay our way.

Gamble is no longer a word in the official lexicon in California. It's *gaming*. Nobody gambles except in illegal gambling joints. We game. Gambling may be a sin; gaming helps reservation economics and the state budget.

Once upon a time, we acted as a community to meet our community needs. We used our taxes to make our lives better. Now, talking about a tax increase is akin to talking about gambling. We don't do it, and if some poor soul is caught using the word, he or she is banished.

Yet gambling is what we are doing with our potential for the future, while our leaders refuse to lead. It's easier to propose cuts to currently under-funded programs, like education and medical care, than it is to present us with a process or program that will result in improvement in the lives of average Americans and their children.

There is a national — maybe international — economic crisis. This has had a negative impact on California's finances and is certainly a restraining factor in approaching the issues delineated above.

Perhaps we are in the midst of a reformulation of that old chestnut, the American dream. Why should our kids do better than we have done? Why should the lives of the poorest among us be our concern? Why should we be concerned that the rich are not only getting richer, but that the gap between them and us is also a growing chasm?

All of the above reflects not only my parents' goals for their children, but also what I learned in the various colleges I attended. As a child of the Depression, I came to understand that if enough of the little folks can get their act together, they can protect their interests and expand our democracy.

Where, oh where, are the truth tellers and the leaders who can articulate the dream and the ways in which it can become reality?

A Visit

Of course, it's a natural phenomenon. Obvious on the face of it (a pun as it turns out). Young folks in expensive private schools are more likely than their public school counterparts to have braces on their teeth.

If you can afford $20,000 tuition, you can sure as hell make sure the kid's teeth are straight.

This less than profound observation comes after another visit to a local private school. I sat in on a seventh-grade social studies class working on presentations for the schoolwide Model United Nations coming up in January. In the spring, a group of students will go to another Model UN — at the United Nations Building in New York City.

The sixteen young intellectuals had each chosen nations they would represent. They took an important global issue and developed a position paper representing their country's position on that problem.

They had done an enormous amount of work using their laptops and other resources. The teacher also told me that both students and parents had mentioned to her that parental international experience and dinner table conversations were a part of the knowledge base.

As they read their statements aloud, I marveled at the amount of knowledge they displayed and the manner in which they had constructed their position papers. The sentences and paragraphs were well constructed, and the vocabulary was extensive and pertinent. Clearly, universities would be beckoning these scholarly young beings.

Discussing all this with the teacher afterwards, I found out that, while they were contemplating world leadership, their current existences were often troubled. Economic difficulties were generating tensions in families, and this was reflected in student behavior. There had even been two fights on campus in the last several weeks.

She noted that her students were now more open in talking about divorces, and there seemed to have been an increase in family breakups. I mentioned that this must be extremely difficult for middle school kids, who are still developing physically and sexually. How do they handle Mom or Dad, or both, now sleeping or cohabiting with someone else?

But these issues were not manifest in this classroom during my one-hour observation. These youngsters were involved in their work and exhibiting a wide range of skills. It was a pleasure to see such active learning.

Two other observations regarding the bodies of these seventh graders. Of the fifteen in class, none of them exhibited the fatness disease that seems to be gripping the United States and some other nations. Exercise? Careful eating?

Size difference and maturation were also quite clear. The girls were tiny to over five feet. Well on the way to womanhood and maybe just awakening to that fact. The boys, too, exhibited a wide range of physical stature. I was almost always the tallest in my classes, which earned me desks in the back of the room, where I could gaze out the window or read what I wanted to read. Cheating on spelling tests was a good deal easier, too.

Cheating. Two still-vivid memories of this particular sin. In my ninth-grade algebra class, I was confronted with a test that went beyond my meager understanding of the process. When the teacher turned her back on the class, I grabbed the test paper from my neighbor across the aisle. It worked. I passed.

In a college midterm, in a large auditorium-like room, I was seated in front of a really, really smart guy. He wrote editorials for the school paper. As I was scribbling away in my blue book, he tapped me on the shoulder and asked for guidance on an essay question. I gave it. I passed. I don't know about him.

Odd I should end up thinking about cheating after my visit to the classroom. These young people, potential inheritors of the universe, are capable and diligent. Why would they ever cheat? Maybe because, at some point, the need to succeed will overwhelm them. Public school or private school, braces or no braces, there are times when we succumb.

The Tie That Binds

We are a diverse nation. Multiple racial groupings, a cacophony of cultures, and many versions of sexuality. What, some people ask, is it that unites us?

A possible response would be the belief in our constitution, the basic document governing our lives. But that seems too abstract, especially today in our politically polarized society.

Our capitalistic freedom to seek and to create personal and family financial security is a possible social glue. But that doesn't quite do it, as we are again betrayed by the business masterminds who gave us the savings and loan breakdown of the 1980s, the high-tech bubble of the 1990s, Enron, and the sordid scandals of the early 2000s. And now the subprime mortgage mess.

We can unite around the brilliance of our scientific achievements that support our economy, improve our standard of living, and attract millions of people from around the world to come here to study and to work.

There are other potential *uniters* tying us together as we wave our flag. International athletic events, such as the Olympics, create support for the teams that represent us. Our generosity to nations suffering through natural disasters as in Somalia and Japan pulls us together in our willingness to assist those in dire need of support.

But in some ways our unity within diversity is a mystery, not only to ourselves but also to the world around us. My friend Diane was sent by our federal government to Armenia's capitol city, Yerevan, to teach a course in school leadership. She found Armenia to be an isolated world, within which ethnic groups remained cloistered entities. Heaven forbid an Armenian marry an Azerbaijani.

In a classroom discussion several weeks into the semester, the class spoke openly about the divisions in their nation. One young lady, who had been to New York City, expressed her amazement at what she found there: "All those languages on the street, the obviously different races and cultures. How can they claim to be American? They're all so different."

A geezer's reaction: after a couple hundred years, we've found out that working and living together makes us stronger than cultural isolation would allow us to be.

It doesn't work all the time. There are still difficulties in inter-group relations, but we work to resolve them. While Armenians won't marry their fellow Armenians who happen to be from a different culture, American cross-cultural marriages are increasing.

Beyond intermarriage, how do we promote — or even find — unity? I don't have a simple answer, but my intuition suggests that, beyond "high-stakes" standards, our schools could do more to make unity within diversity an important priority.

Chaos and Sainthood

She's a gray-haired African American lady. Someone, maybe me, should be filling out her application for preliminary sainthood.

She serves as principal of a school created to serve sixth-, seventh-, and eighth- graders who have exhibited behavior problems in other schools.

As her field supervisor, I was to meet with the principal while she completed her administrative credential program at a local college. Before she was assigned to the school, she had been a summer-school principal, her only on-site administrative experience.

It's an old building that previously served as an elementary school. It's in a middle-class neighborhood of mostly small, single-family homes.

I went to the office, which was close to the school entrance. There were four students in the outer office along with a clerk. The principal was involved in a parent conference in her office. The clerk let her know I was there and told me it would be a few minutes.

Fifty minutes, eight students, three teachers, and four parents later, we sat down to talk. There were still two parents and three students waiting to meet with her.

I suggested she had more important things to do than talk with me. She waved that idea aside saying with a sigh, "I need a break." And how! The fifty minutes observing had been a circus of game playing and power testing, childish behavior at once comic and tragic.

Set piece one. Because students had been using their cell phones in class, the principal collected the phones, promising to return them at the end of the day. One girl, who had been late to class, refused. The principal brought her to the office and asked her again. "No!"

"All right, you'll be suspended for the day, and I'll call your mother to come in tomorrow."

More no's. Three more students came in. There were now five in the room, plus a parent who went into the principal's office with her to talk about another student.

The clerk called the cell phone girl's mother. The girl talked to her, pleading to keep her phone. At the same time, another girl was throwing faux punches at two boys in between chewing on the drawstring of her sweatshirt. The clerk and two teachers who came in kept telling her to sit down.

In the hallway just outside the open door, teachers, students, and support staff mingled and talked loudly enough to disrupt the disruption in the office.

Finally the telephone war ended with the surrender of the phone, and the miscreant went off to class even though the principal had suspended her.

Set piece two. A teacher brought in a male student who had not been doing his work, along with the evidence — several sheets of paper with questions that had not been answered. He claimed he'd done what he should have done. The teacher left the papers with the clerk and asked her to see that he did his work.

Another test of wills, with no end to the issue. He was still refusing when I left the school.

Set piece three. More testing. This young man had been sent to the office for refusing to take off his red cap. Multiple requests came from the clerk and the principal, who came out of her second parent meeting. Back and forth it went. "Why do you want my hat? You can't have my hat. It belongs to me," etc.

Finally the clerk asked him to come up to the counter that separated her from her visitors. She whispered something to him and grabbed his hat.

Now his refrain began with, "You can't do that. Gimme back my hat."

And as a backdrop, the pretend fighter practiced her moves with another boy who had come in.

I couldn't help but laugh to myself at all the foolishness, and then saw the tragedy as these young people created their future.

In my discussion with the principal she told me, again, that only one of her six teachers is committed to these kids and holds them to some level of academic expectations. This, she says, is the biggest part of her problem, along with the family situations of her students. She hopes to recruit some new staff for spring.

With a small enrollment, this is an expensive operation. The per-pupil expenditure, including an $80,000 counseling contract, runs over $12,000 per pupil. In the state of California, the average figure is $7,415.

Unfortunately, the school's enrollment is almost all African American and Latino. These two groups constitute the largest components of California's dropouts.

The district is trying to provide these young people with an education and the consequent improvement in their chances at some measure of success in life. The chaos that I observed today was an enormous waste in terms of money and damaged lives.

Wanting to do the right thing is not enough. Perhaps the schools cannot do the job. We need — the nation needs — to find a way to provide these young people with the knowledge, skills, and behaviors that lead to constructive lives. But first we have to get their attention.

And we can't leave it up to the saints of the world. There are just a few of them, and at some point they get worn out.

Wasting the Future

There is a lot of waste in America. The thousands of landfills across the nation are methane-leaking testimony to our extravagance.

Our most dangerous waste occurs because of several of our social policies. One flows from the "drug wars" and the many thousands of people, mostly under thirty-five, who are stacked in our prisons at a cost of between $35,000 and $50,000 a year.

In a similar situation involving unanticipated outcomes, the "three strikes" legislation that has been in vogue over the last fifteen years or so sometimes results in nonviolent criminals serving life terms. The financial drain on those outside the jails is bad enough, but the real waste occurs in the lives of those who have been put there. What are they to do for a livelihood upon their release? How will their convictions impact their futures, as well as those of their families?

So there we have two very obvious examples of ways in which we commit social waste. The money spent on incarceration could be used to achieve numerous social goals. The unfulfilled promise in the lives of those jailed could provide a source of workers, ideas, and stable families.

There is, however, a more hidden waste that impinges on the lives of our young folks. The idea put forth in a recent issue of *The American Prospect* seemed a bit far-fetched. But on second thought caused me to gesture emphatically with two thumbs up. The concept: our current processes for college admission (which include high school grades, SAT, achievements in nonacademic areas, and family characteristics) are too restrictive and close off college and university admission for many who would succeed in these environments. And there is evidence to support this contention.

The author cites several studies in support of his idea. I'll note only one of them. Conducted by former presidents of Harvard and Princeton, this research revealed that students enrolled under "affirmative action programs graduated and proceeded to earn advanced degrees at the same rate as a reference group of other students matched to the affirmative-action admits."

In other words, there is a mass of educable, trainable talent out there that is being limited in both aspirations and achievements, based upon faulty assumptions. That means that those folks in the second and third tiers in my junior high school class were as capable as I.

We all knew the classrooms in which the better students did their thing. We were the chosen, the ninth grade winners in the race to the college of our choice.

A third thought intrudes. In my undergraduate years at Berkeley, the campus was loaded with ex-military folks on the GI Bill. Several whom I knew said that, absent this support, they would never have even thought about going to a university. It was the ex-GIs who made possible the enormously successful American economy of the 1950s and '60s.

Today, fifteen nations — almost all of Western Europe plus Australia and Korea — have a higher percentage of young people who are more likely to earn a bachelor's degree than are youthful Americans. This is not a portent of American success in an increasingly competitive world.

Other social factors combine to exacerbate the restrictiveness of our higher education system. Chief among them is the decline in public financial support for colleges and universities. This has been brought about by the failure of states to generate tax dollars to keep up with the inflation of educational costs, as well as the current deep recession that has created enormous strains on state budgets.

As always, we are confronted with Americans who are ready and eager to claim that we're number one. But as is the case with medical care, this is just a fantasy. A fantasy we'll pay for in the years ahead.

❖ ❖ ❖

A Capitalist of Note

It was an opportunity I don't often get, so I signed on for a trip into memory land with someone who believed I had been a "significant" person in her high school career.

My meeting with her came about because her younger sister had been part of a group of high school classmates who put together a thirty-year class reunion. I was one of the six teachers and administrators they invited to share the festivities.

In a pre-dinner discussion, the sister told me, "Jane would love to see you." With that, she gave me an announcement of Jane's upcoming inauguration as president of an important county business association, with the telephone number written on the back.

So I promised I'd call, even though my memories of Jane were vague and possibly confused with three or four other young ladies. We arranged to meet at a Borders. I was early and bought a decaffeinated coffee and tried to find a vacant table. After a couple of minutes a mother and her preschool daughter began to move out, and I grabbed their spot.

Jane arrived and came over to the table. She recognized me, but I certainly did not recognize her. She got herself some tea, and we began to talk.

We spent a good bit of time talking about her life after high school. While she was now, in her own words, "a capitalist," she attached the words "liberal" and "progressive" to the noun. An unusual but certainly not unheard of label.

Our discussion touched on the influences in her life. It was clear she recognized family was central, and in the center of the center was education. Her parents were immigrants from the Philippines, and her dad died the year she entered high school. Jane earned a bachelor's in sociology from the University of California, Davis, and an M.A. in education from San Francisco State.

After a few years in education, and at a time very much like today when state funding for schools was in the tank, she challenged herself to succeed in a career in real estate. Now she is a power in her profession, conducting seminars throughout the nation and playing a major role in working out her county's future.

Incidentally, her brother and sister have also been quite successful. He was a pilot in the military, retiring as a major, and has been flying for Northwest Airlines. She has a Ph.D. from Cal in public health.

And so, I asked, after about a half an hour, "What did I do that influenced you so much?"

She had been in a civics class during my last year at the high school. During a lively classroom discussion, she had said something, neither of us could remember what, and I had banished her to the closet in the room. The next day she assumed leadership of a protest movement with banners and slogans on the blackboard demanding free speech. After a few days and before the Christmas holiday, the protest simmered down.

Free speech and constitutional rights became the centerpiece of our classroom work. For Jane, leading the protest had been a totally new experience and a part of her emergence as a "progressive, liberal capitalist."

Was that what I meant to do?

WE CAN DO BETTER

I have never been arrested for prostitution. Nor have I ever prostituted myself — though I came close once — for financial gain because of an official position that I held.

Neither do I hold any great animus towards those poor young women and men who feel they must sell their bodies to survive. Life has its ugly aspects.

Maybe that's why many of America's great universities have sought and found street corners where they can display their wares to entice the fat wallets to enter their houses.

Sadly, for me and some alumni from my generation, the University of California has become an active participant in this enterprise.

Yes, the university is in big financial trouble. The mega recession and the mega-mega state budget shortfall are a major part of the problem. The budget is bedeviled with the unforeseen outcomes of voters' choices, the decline in state revenues, and misplaced priorities. For example, ten percent of the budget goes for prisons; higher education gets about seven percent.

Thus, university administrators have been driven to search for additional funding. That money is readily available from two sources: out-of-state students, who are charged premium tuition to attend California's colleges and universities, and foreign students who also pay extra for the privilege of learning in the tarnished Golden State.

That's fair.

Eligible students from California may be denied entry because of the arrival of the visitors. What businessperson would turn his or her back on the extra bucks needed to reinforce the UC system's ability to support itself? Nonresident tuition is just over $22,000, while resident fees to the university are $10,781.

California schools are not alone in this form of fund-raising. It goes on all across the country. A goodly number of U.S. universities have opened overseas sites using professors from the home campus. This, of course, limits the number of American students who can partake of the learning and wisdom of the traveling professorate.

Another revenue enhancer comes from that form of the entertainment world labeled intercollegiate athletics. Within this budget category, the gold is found in lucrative television contracts.

The various universities have traditionally organized themselves into conferences, such as the Big Ten, the PAC Ten, the Southeast Conference, the Big Sky Conference, and so on.

Football and, in some instances, basketball have attracted substantial alumni and public support. The money brought in goes to fund the entire athletic program at the schools. When games are televised, the schools playing the conference and its member institutions share the proceeds.

The proliferation of cable television channels now provides a much greater opportunity for TV exposure. The television folks look for schools that will attract audiences, and they make offers to the various conferences. The universities look at these offers and can exercise a choice — stay in the same old group or find a new home with a better TV deal. So the Big Ten has evolved into the Big Eleven, soon to be the Big Twelve; the PAC Ten will become the PAC Twelve. This buck searching goes on down the athletic food chain, and smaller schools get involved.

Athletic conferences have not been permanent conglomerates. When I was a kid (remember Tom Harmon?) the Coast Conference included Idaho and Montana. Good-bye to them, a long time ago, and hello to Arizona and Arizona State and soon, too, to Colorado.

I have nothing against colleges and universities. I was an inhabitant for many years and even now have a minimal responsibility at a very fine school. It's just that the street corner act is tawdry and well below how our palaces of learning should behave.

Let's get on with educating our citizens. We, the public, benefit; we, the public, should pay the freight.

An Idea for Schools

Once in a while, I rummage in our household office and find some interesting stuff. At least I think it's interesting.

It happened again on the first Monday in October. There was a yellow file under a pile of other stuff, and for some reason, I picked it up and wandered through the contents.

I found several items that I had written a few years ago. Maybe thirty or thirty-five years ago, to be more exact. Geezers have the right, even the responsibility, to resurface their work when it might be interesting or useful.

My concern then, as it is now, was: how do schools adjust the seemingly unchanging realities of school functioning to reflect the dynamism inherent in a rapidly transforming world?

In 1967, Dr. Robert J. Schaefer of Columbia University wrote *The School as a Center of Inquiry*. This, and some other reading I had done, spurred my thinking about schools and schooling.

Since World War II, the United States and the rest of the world have been going through a seemingly unending revolution of rising expectations. If we have little or nothing, we expect to have something; if we have lots or almost everything, we expect more. Education has been both a spur to this revolution and one of its goals.

An increasingly important element in the revolution has been rapid technological change. The Internet and its various permutations provide instant knowledge and communication — as well as instant nonsense, opinions, and misinformation.

Indiscriminate use of such technology adds to the pervasive breakdowns in respect for and belief in established authority and social institutions — including questioning the relevance of those institutions. For educators, this has meant increasing debate about schools, what they are, and what they should be.

There is a self-replicating set of behaviors that marks the life of the school person. Things are done, organization is created, and rewards are dispensed so as to ensure that those who model the traditional and acceptable continue things as they are and were meant to be. Spontaneity and excitement fall by the wayside.

It has been generally accepted that schools exist to educate young people for their lives in the future. But while the future has always been unknowable, the uncertainty seems even greater today. We are faced with continuing economic problems, along with the potential of global terrorism and the increasing power and rising political and economic power of China, India, and Brazil. These concerns have generated new questions related to our schools today — and in the future. What is the meaning of schooling in 2010 and the years ahead?

The need to answer this question is the generative force behind my notion of an alternative educational form. Such a search must involve the total staff of middle and high schools, as well as the students and communities of which they are a part.

For schools to function successfully as centers of inquiry, four preconditions have to be met. In the first place, there must be an awareness of their problems and the willingness to seek new definitions and new solutions. Second, there must be a sense of pride and a desire for success among the staff and the community. Third, greater openness is needed in the relationship between the school and its community. Fourth, a certain "spirit of the place" must be established to sanction and promote change and those who make it.

While functioning as a center of inquiry, the school's primary objective is to provide a climate for school change, demonstrating how secondary schools can become better places to work and learn as change becomes an institutional norm.

Two lesser aims follow from this central point. First, school personnel will be provided access to research results and will be trained in research skills and problem-solving techniques. This will allow them to adapt the results of current research in education to the needs of their particular schools. They can also tailor powerful research results to the problems originally identified. Second, school personnel will be given tools to help them develop new solutions to existing problems on their own. Innovation will begin with teachers in the classroom, based on their perspective on the educative function as a problem to be defined and solved.

This research emphasis (both original and derivative) will lead to several outcomes:

1) The school organization itself will be restructured so as to be a more effective problem-solving mechanism — and to allow the institutionalization of change processes, as well as the results of research and innovations arising in the project.
2) Emphasis will be placed on participatory processes in decision making, enabling administrators, school boards, and the community-at-large to have a stake in the implementation of project work and the direction it takes.
3) There will be greater reliance on using community resources to support the school.
4) The school will generate its own master plan for education.
5) Teachers will become actively engaged in developing their own curriculum and curriculum materials, as an outgrowth of the research undertaken.
6) Using all the knowledge we can muster, we will demonstrate that schools can accept and accommodate innovation.

A school functioning as a center of inquiry presupposes several things: a community deeply concerned and involved in its school; a staff willing to examine itself, its role, and its skills in the light of changing demands; the administration and faculty's desire for increased competence in problem definition and solution; and, most important, the sense that something can be done to bring meaning and order out of the chaos engulfing society.

These conditions are by no means impossible to realize. There are schools operating today that, with a shift in emphasis and effort, could undertake the endeavor. The risks are not great when measured against current accomplishments. The potential rewards for young people and for school staffs are enormous.

At the very least, the school functioning as a center of inquiry might bring some fun and some intellectual joy to the schoolhouse.

SPORTS

Sports, like politics, has its winners and losers. But as I was growing up, whether our local teams won or lost, our family followed them closely. First and foremost was the San Francisco Seals baseball team. My brother and I would sometimes go to the Sunday double header after completing Sunday School. I was chosen to be Sports Editor of the Lincoln Log, my high school newspaper. At the University of California, I held the same position at the Daily Californian. You don't get concussions from typing, but participating in sports is a physical activity. Along with the thrill of victory, there is agony of defeat. Following the ups and downs of the San Francisco Giants, the 49ers, and my tennis, I have gained other insights.

A Journey to Redemption

It was bloody awful. Nothing but personal failure leading to the failure of my partners, who generously refused to condemn my performance and even invited me to participate in next Tuesday's matches.

Tennis is not life. Constantly botched backhands, volleys flying by the end line, and lobs that were far too short are simply manifestations of athletic ineptitude. They are only tangentially related to my worth as a person. And I have proof — there are all those things I've done, the books and articles, the offices I've held, and the successful kids and grandkids. So I've never won a tennis tournament — hell, I've never really entered a real tournament.

But somehow, my travails on the court create a cloud that surrounds me for hours after the post-match shower. Every now and then, I convince myself I'm playing better. I'm on a real upswing, so to speak. Ah, the joys of self-deception.

While my worth as a tennis player resembles that of many third-world countries' currencies, there is gold in those reminiscences from my real life that blow away the tennis-induced cloud. Yet memories are not sufficient. There is still the need to do and to be involved in the world around me and, ultimately, to be valued for my contribution.

The search for self-esteem is our current analogue for the great California gold rush of the nineteenth century. Kids today can feast on the baubles and trophies freely dispensed by the schools and leagues in which they perform. For the more academic, there are certificates and other documentation signifying achievement. You do not have to win, be part of a winning team, or score the highest on academic tests. You are awarded something you can put on a shelf or a wall. It's not that you're OK — you're an award winner — a participant. (An article in the *San Francisco Chronicle* reads, "Self-esteem has run rampant, study says.")

OK — I'm sort of bitter. Our walls, even the walls in our office, are filled with the terrific photographs my wife has taken on our various trips. Surely there should be something recognizing my achievements in a variety of fields, but do I need them? These are the memories I can pull up:

- The time I saw a book I had edited on a library bookshelf
- The lovely words spoken at my several retirement parties
- The joy involved in our children's and grandchildren's success
- And more, much, much more

And then there was today. Sharply hit volleys, well-hit backhand returns of serve, winning service games, and then the resurgence of my best shot — the forehand return.

Yes! I'm OK — you're OK. Let's have a beer so we can arrange our next match.

REMINISCENCE ONE

Springtime. Gentle showers, daffodils, green hills, and baseball. The sports pages and the TV begin to display the antics of the soon-to-be heroes or bums as they endeavor to get ready for their season. Predictions abound about which major league team will make it through the long season and into the playoffs leading to the World Series.

All of today's hoopla brings back memories of my introduction to the professional sport as a nine- or ten-year-old. In 1940, we moved into San Francisco to a flat owned by one of my aunts at Twenty-fourth and Folsom streets. This turned out to be only twelve blocks from Seals Stadium, home of the resident nine, the Seals.

The Seals played in the Pacific Coast League, which was one step below the Majors — the National and American Leagues. Players in the three Triple-A leagues were aspiring major leaguers or veterans of the majors on their way to retirement.

I think I was fooling with our radio one day when I encountered the Seals in the person of Ernie Smith, their broadcaster. "There he is on first, safe as a Silvertown [or something like that]," Smith intoned, referring to a base runner and his sponsor in the same phrase. Soon, I began to seek out the broadcasts and follow the team in the *Examiner* sports page.

There were players of note: "Nanny" Fernandez at shortstop; Joe Sprinz, the catcher who lost most of his teeth trying to catch a ball dropped from the Tower of the Sun at the Treasure Island World Fair; "Sad" Sam Gibson, pitcher; Win "Pard" Ballou, relief pitcher; manager Lefty O'Doul; and lots more.

The season wore on and ended, and it was "Wait till next year." And next year proved to be different for me. Our family went to a game early in the season, and I got to see what I had heard and read about. It was a revelation, and it led to a deal.

I could sweep the three flights of stairs in our building and the street in front of it for enough money to go to a game, buy an Eskimo Pie, and a program. Thirty cents. I could easily walk to the stadium, so Saturday afternoon became baseball time.

What do I remember?

Not much in terms of hits and errors. I found out that the wind coming over the right-field fence could be strong and cold. I heard the players curse a lot. Screaming at umpires was fun. A pleasure to yell at O'Doul, "You Marblehead!"

In terms of personal contacts, there was "Danny," the Eskimo Pie guy. He followed a set route through the stands, lugging his cooler and hollering out the name of his product. Almost twenty years later, I saw him at Candlestick Point while watching a Giants game. He was still selling chocolate covered ice cream.

There were the gamblers betting on the outcome of the game, whether a hitter would get on base, and anything else they chose to contest. I sat in the upper grandstand in left field, beyond third base, and the gamblers were several sections toward home plate. Sometimes I could hear their wagers and see the cash change hands.

After a couple of games, I learned how to keep score. So I had to bring a pencil, or it would cost me another nickel to buy one.

What does it all mean? Nothing. But there I was, ten years old, walking the twelve blocks to the game by myself.

Nothing epochal, but I did it!

An Affair of the Heart

It was in 1948, I think, that my dad first bought tickets for the San Francisco 49ers' football season. Each Sunday for six or seven years, our family church was Kezar Stadium in Golden Gate Park.

For almost sixty years, I have followed the fortunes and misfortunes of the Niners. Good years, bad years, I was there for them. In most cases, "there" was in front of our TV, where I began to predict how my weeks would go based on the performance of the team on Sunday. If they did well, success awaited me Monday through Saturday.

There have been plenty of low points in my relationship with the San Francisco eleven, but the lows were obliterated by their first Super Bowl victory when the town went nuts. People came out of their houses cheering; drivers honked their horns; bartenders poured. Hooray!

But today in 2007 we are below a low. The team stinks. The fan base watches for a quarter or a half and then grabs the remote control. Who can watch the ineptitude on parade wearing the gold and red? If I had not matured and still believed in the power of the 49er mojo, I would not be able to get out of bed on the day after another desultory performance by my former heroes.

Am I being unfaithful? Now, in their hour of need, is there a heroic deed in me that could bring some surcease from the sorrow in which they wallow? Any good, healthy relationship is based on equality, with both sides contributing to the success of their endeavor. Have I been lacking? What could I have done?

The answers to the above questions are, of course, no, no, no, and nothing.

In the beginning, I was seduced. There they were — Frankie Albert, Alyn Beals, Horm Standlee, Johnny Stryzkalsky, et al. — luring me into a commitment that would survive almost sixty years. Enough already.

Now I can be free. Sunday is mine, not theirs. We can travel to Monterey, go to the theater, visit family, or read all of the paper with the TV off. Such a relief!

Yet the agony of defeat is somehow outweighed by the hope of the impending victory: the sense that, this time, it will be different — that within those noble uniforms hearts will again beat with the strength that comes with triumph.

Lots of luck. The team stinks. . . But wait a minute — No, wait four years — Now 9 wins and 1 loss in 2011: Sunday trips are cancelled again!

A Diagnosis

It is a nice crosscourt forehand. Al is moving to the net, but my shot, low and hard, is too much for him to handle. Score: 15–30.

Two minutes later, maybe three, the match is over. I limp off the court to my car, about fifty yards away, the pain in my right leg too much for me to continue.

Within a week, I'm in the doctor's office. "Sciatica," she says and arranges an appointment with a therapist. He walks me down to his office, where I quickly find out that I am very bent over as I walk and that my back is largely immobile. Standing up straight is a pain — a very real pain. There follows an introduction to the exercise regimen that will be my companion for a long, undetermined time.

More visits to the therapist. More exercise. I stand taller. The pain calms down. We're off to Hawaii for some snorkeling. After several trials, it works OK.

This is all new to me. I've had a couple of broken bones, a touch of tennis elbow, and some aches and pains that didn't require medical attention. Well, there was a sore shoulder several years ago and some prescribed exercises. Lasted about two weeks.

This is different.

I have always been the classic white guy — slow and can't jump. Now I am slower — almost cemented to the ground. Sometimes I can lurch a bit and make a shot. The serve, never great, is OK, and my forehand return of serve is a winning weapon. Naturally, folks learn to hit to my backhand.

This goes on for a year and a half. No change. Then my daughter looks up sciatica on Google. It's supposed to last six weeks.

Doctor time again. X-rays, then an MRI. And panic city. The nurses lay me down, and I slide into what could be a torpedo. "Keep your eyes closed and remain still."

They hand me a little emergency signal device if I want out. Then the noise begins — bang, bang, bang, bang...I want out. *Claustrophobized.* Scared. No way, José.

Most embarrassing, but there is a second chance at another facility where they use a more open machine. Fortified by a couple of Valium and with my wife driving the thirty miles to the tormenting machine, I am ready. "Keep your eyes closed and remain still."

There is pain in my right buttock. I wiggle a bit to relieve it. Dumb. After I spend an hour in the noisemaker, the technician cuts it off. "No useful picture. You moved too much."

A week later, once more into the imaging machine. Success. A useful picture. A diagnosis. Spinal stenosis — a degenerative condition involving arthritis.

Spinal anything sounds bad to me. My wife had back surgery in 1963 and then again in 2006. There is pain — real pain — involved in that. However, there are options, and there will be no immediate decision.

But question number one is: do I go on a trip to Peru and the headwaters of the Amazon three months from now? Our daughter had been after me to go to the doctor, as my "sciatica" continued to cause me to limp and bend over when I walked (it wasn't as bad as you said, was my rejoinder).

Now she lets me know the real choice. "Do you want to surrender to the condition or continue to live an engaged and interesting life?"

In essence, she's saying, "Go for it."

My physician is ill, so I make an appointment to see her substitute (I must forget for the moment how I and my classmates treated substitute teachers when I was in high school). There are questions I, actually we, need answered.

In short, the answer is — keep doing what you're doing. Exercise, tennis, walking, and keeping positive.

Thus, the long prelude leads to an inconclusive but heartening admonition. It's kind of "You ain't over till you're over, and for now you're in charge of that."

It's funny how much you can build on a few little words.

What's the Score?

Tennis courts are for playing games, scoring points, winning, losing, and a kind of social camaraderie. Fun, in other words.

Sometimes, simple things like games can evolve into more complex forms of interaction. So it was late last week in one of our over-the-hill gang's doubles matches.

Mike and I had lost the first set 4-6 but won number two 9-7 when we spent a few minutes talking during the change of courts. A bad joke or two, an observation on the skills of the players on the other court, and then Bill, a proactive sort, said something about the Democrat's primary battle in the crawl to the presidency. This comment touched a nerve or two in Dave's political consciousness.

"How can anyone even think of voting for one of them? They just want to raise taxes and start new programs. It would cost me an additional $3,500. And if they raised the capital gains tax to 25 percent, it would be much worse, and the economy would be worse off than it is today." (The remarks quoted have been sanitized.)

Well, this diatribe captured my attention and transferred my competitive energies from tennis to the battle for social good.

"So we pay more taxes — big deal. At some point we have to handle the debt, and there are some troubling social needs we must take care of."

"Oh," says he. "Like what?"

"Medical care, for one."

"You're crazy. We have the best medical care in the world."

This pushed me further along the road to righteousness. I did, after all, know something about the issue beyond the Michael Moore movie, which I had enjoyed. The numbers were on my side — life expectancy, infant mortality, the costs, the health gap between rich and poor, the international research that ranked the United States below most of the western world. We were decidedly somewhere south of the best.

At this point, our partners took to the court telling us, in effect, to shut up and get on with the match. We did.

While there were no blows struck and civility reigned through the conclusion of our play, I was a wee bit disturbed as I drove the fifteen miles to my shower and lunch.

Somehow, two grown men with a combined age over 130 had engaged in a discussion on a very serious matter and had succeeded in babbling past one another. Each of us was secure in the belief that he held the correct view.

Yes, we had babbled, and one of the other players had mentioned something about the Tower of Babel. Later in the day, I looked it up. According to Genesis 11:4-9, people in the ancient city of Shinar tried to build a tower to reach heaven. They were forced to give up the job because of the confusion of their languages.

Dave and I were both speaking English, but our language was unintelligible to us as we talked. This is no way to build a tower or to work through serious disagreements about how we live with one another.

Communication in tennis is much easier. I blast a return of serve crosscourt and he returns into the net; Dave sends one of my weak backhands up the middle past me and my partner. We can make a point a damn sight easier than we can make sense to one another.

A Career Path?

I enjoy sports. I've never been any good at the playing thing, but I've had fun watching all manner of sporting contests and even made a few bucks doing it.

A long time ago, in a city on the eastern shore of the Bay, I was a sports writer and editor for the *Daily Californian,* which claimed to have the largest circulation of any morning daily in the East Bay. Actually, we weren't a daily. We published five days a week.

I had been the sports editor of the unesteemed *Lincoln Log,* my high school newspaper. Entering Cal, I had no thoughts about establishing a career in journalism. In fact, I was picked out of the registration line by two big guys who told me I was the perfect size to be an oarsman on the Cal crew. Trips to the Olympics were a sure thing. Just sign up and become a part of the greatest crew on earth. They got my signature.

They didn't tell me about the hours and hours of very hard work, three days a week and sometimes on Saturday. I lasted a semester and, although I was invited back, I decided to look elsewhere for my athletic glory.

So back to the typewriter I went — and up through the ranks from scribe to night editor to assistant editor to editor. The latter two spots paid beer money. Then the Associated Press needed a "stringer" on campus, and a martini or two became possible.

We covered the gambit of athletic events, from intramural contests among a variety of campus organizations to national championships, like the NCAA track meet. It was great fun, and I worked with some good folks, including Ron Fimrite, who went on to fame and fortune with the *San Francisco Chronicle* and *Sports Illustrated.*

All of the above was generated by attendance at this year's Cal-UCLA football game. Almost every year since graduation, we (my wife — the Stanford grad — and I) have gone to the "Big Game," the annual Cal-Stanford battle. In recent years, my brother has taken us to one other game per year.

While at Cal, I also managed to go to enough classes to garner a degree in political science. To "garner a gonfalon" was then a sports cliché for winning a game or a championship. Thus, my garnering was limited to the academic part of university life.

Recently it has come to my attention that the current (till January 20, 2009) administration in D.C. has linked my two Cal lives and shone a light on a path I could have taken upon graduation.

The Decider in Chief made clear, some years ago, that he would love the job of Commissioner of Baseball. He has already been an owner of a major league team and being commissioner would make him the model for the sports-politics leader.

His secretary of state, Condoleezza Rice, has said that she would love to be the chief executive of the National Football League. Not likely to happen, but possible.

One major hurdle for both of them is their record as losers. They were granted the opportunity to make the USA a winner in the international game, but they have failed miserably. It must be said that Rice, in the last years, has shown more skill and gained more success than her boss.

Being the chief of a sports league is a bit easier than leading the nation. All you have to do is provide for the owners to get more money.

Problem one: the Bush economy.

LIFE AS IT IS LIVED

I've been sick the last week. Nothing serious — a bad cough, a nose running better than Sea Biscuit, and an almost total lack of energy.

A couple of days ago, I went to a luncheon meeting and came home exhausted. I told my wife that I didn't understand my body's reaction. Her response went beyond the three words I repeat here, "At your age…"

And so I responded. "At my age? What has that got to do with anything?"

A lot. Two weeks before the cold, I had my prostate biopsied for possible cancer. Enlarged prostate, a product of age. No cancer.

Then there was the wound on the front of my right shoulder. It wasn't healing. What was it? Dermatologist time. It's a precancerous condition to be treated with an ointment. Call back in four months.

Just stuff happening.

So today it was "Let's give it a try" day. Off to the courts in Burlingame for old fools doubles. My daughter, the nurse, advised against it, with a tone of voice that said "You'll be sorry."

I did get tired. Some muscles ached. I didn't get through two full sets before dizziness set in. I was not sorry.

Managed to hit some good returns — even a couple of backhands — as well as some winning forehands down the middle and one really good volley. Serves were a bit off.

To have ended sorry would have been to put aside the advice for living proffered by my granddaughter, the barrister. On being asked about some difficult things going on in her ultra-busy life, she said, "Remember, I'm a half-full person, unlike my parents."

Half full or half empty — that's how we view our beer mugs. For those of us who focus on the empty, there is soon to be a choice — do we order up another one before we hit the road?

For the half-full gang, the choice is delayed while they savor the content of their glass.

So as I toddled onto the court, I was looking longingly at the glass, ready to decide. And as I returned the first serve with a medium-good forehand, it was clear. Half full.

Staying in the Game

Yesterday I retired.

After one set, the back pain seemed to grow worse despite the pill I had ingested earlier. Better to accept the reality represented by my spinal stenosis than to risk injury.

My court partners accepted the decision gracefully, even though my weakness botched up their morning. I, on the other hand, was less than kind and accepting in my display of weakness. Punishment was what I needed. A pain to match my pain.

What better pain producer than a good dose of guilt. "Look what you've done to those good souls who got up early expecting to get their three sets in. You've got to call them and apologize more than you just did. Damn it! Get your lousy act together."

And much worse, all for thirty minutes on the road home.

Through the afternoon, my back simmered down, and I did what I needed to do without depending on my newly purchased cane. The tennis guys didn't know about this acquisition — I wasn't about to share my decrepitude. A cane! How can you play tennis with a cane?

Well, you can't. But if the back and the leg aren't producing any pain, you don't need the cane, and it's still possible to hit a good forehand.

That evening I had to attend a meeting in Redwood City. I'm on a county committee that approves or disapproves petitions to change school district boundaries. It's a twenty-five-mile drive in a drizzle. A bit worrisome, and as I maneuver south on 280, the leg begins to ache.

Arriving at the County Office of Education, I left the cane in the car. I can walk without it, though I do limp.

After three and a half hours, the committee voted, as I hoped it would, to deny the petition before it. I had taken an active part in the discussion and believed my contributions were helpful.

Walking to my car with one of the committee members, the limp was gone. I could have (but didn't) sort of run to my vehicle. The good guys had won one; truth and beauty had prevailed; the American way of life was safe. It felt so good.

Parenthetically, the meeting was an example of civil political discourse in a land where incivility has apparently become the norm. There was a diversity of views expressed over four meetings, and we could still smile at one another and acknowledge valid points as they were made. Community democracy.

So the day ended well with its downs and ups and a couple of lessons relearned.

It's time to give up the false bravado related to my bad leg. Keep playing but when you feel the pain, it's time to sit. "Take the painkillers and keep active," the doctor said. So do it, and don't think you're kidding anyone.

Then there's the mind-over-body experience after the evening meeting. Good stuff — the success at decision making — can push aside pain.

Today, the sore back has reappeared but in a diminished state. I carted the newly clean laundry from downstairs up to the bedroom. Took garbage down to the garage. Put the garden tools away.

Feeling good. A one-loss, one-win day. And a couple of lessons to be filed away.

Enjoying the Moment

The wine flowed, the food tasted fine, the chatter was sprinkled with laughter, and a good time was had by all.

'Twas the annual, sometimes semiannual, gathering of our tennis group, this time augmented by the widow of one of our gang. Five of us had our wives with us. David's wife died two years ago.

With no, absolutely no, disrespect intended, this essay will focus on the male contingent at the table. Over the years, from the 1970s, we and about twenty others had swatted tennis balls at one another.

David, now ninety, was part of our creation. He does not play now because of several physical problems. Dion has the second longest tenure and he, too, is on the retired list because of his health.

Our principal courts, at the start, were located on the campus of a Catholic girls' high school in the Burlingame Hills. Our stay there may have been prolonged because the aunt of one of our players had given the school $5,000 via her will. We don't know if this had anything to do with their putting up with us on Sunday mornings, but it became part of our mythology.

I had joined the entourage in the late seventies. Al and Bill showed up in the eighties and Tom in the nineties.

While we are Caucasoid and three of us spent much of our working lives in public schools, there is diversity within our ranks. Al was a truck driver, Bill a pharmacist, and Tom an insurance executive who spent a good number of years working in Europe.

Politically, our range is conservative to progressive, but we don't go there very often. Keep the warfare on the courts where we can have actual winners.

We are competitors. We want to win our matches. We are careful on our line calls and often will grant an additional serve, if the first or second serve bounces off the backstop and ends up close to the court, where it presents a hazard to a player moving back to smash an overhead. Gentlemen are us.

Over the decades, there have been one or two guys who have joined us who did not exhibit the high degree of rectitude we prize in our troop. One fellow became notorious for giving himself the advantage on his calls. He also became infamous for his reluctance to contribute new balls to our games.

The four remaining players at the table all have, or have had, a variety of accidents, strains, and pains that have kept us from competing in the U.S. Open. Bill is the best player, and he has difficulty with his right eye. Al often wears support for his injured legs. Tom once hurt his shoulder badly on court and has recently had cataract surgery. I have my spinal stenosis, which further limits my already limited mobility. The goal for all of us is to keep on keeping on.

A day of playing badly is a bummer for each of us. On those days on which the shots are dropping, even an unexpected bill in the mail will not threaten the joy within.

David says that he dreams about tennis a couple of times a week. It is a reminder that he can no longer play the game he enjoyed so much.

His experience causes me to wonder what it will be like for me when my racket is put away. I'll certainly have more time to write my little essays, but I'll have less to write about. The reunions will continue, but there will be more talk in the past tense. Will there be dreams to remind me of what once was?

I'm not quite ready to find the answer to that question.

Two Dreams

Some American dreams live on.

It became tangible in the first week of November 2010. First the San Francisco Giants won the World Series. The lowly, all-pitch, no-hit, slow-moving Giants dispatched the reigning National League Champions to make it to the World Series. They then froze the steamy bats of the Texas Rangers in the series. Who could have thunk it in March or even in August?

What kind of team was this — a bunch of over-the-hill types with young pitchers? Then mid-season a rookie catcher, who looked to be fifteen or sixteen, came up and performed in a very unrookie-like manner. Cool beyond his years. Then other players were picked up as the season wore on.

But it was clear to most of the baseball prognosticators that the Giants were not up to their opponents in their ability. Maybe wait till next year but certainly not in 2010.

The second big dream scene was the electoral debut of something called the Tea Party. Beginning in the summer of 2009 at town hall meetings across the country, they made their presence known, protesting the president's medical care program, the increasing size and role of government, and their taxes.

Waving flags and wearing tri-corner hats, some of them with tea bags dangling, the Tea Partiers intended to focus the nation on the rebellion against British taxation prior to the Revolutionary War. So the Boston Tea Party became parent to its twenty-first-century child.

The Tea Party didn't win the 2010 congressional election, but its supporters were a major factor in some of the Republican victories across the nation. Democrats point out three dry tea bags — Delaware, Nevada, and Colorado — as evidence that the Republicans may need something stronger than tea if their message is to prevail in the future.

So from November 1 through November 3, two disparaged, laughed-at organizations took center stage in American life. One was victorious; the other displayed the potential to move American politics further to the right. Work hard, play by the rules, and you can make people believers.

That's what we have now, as we reach the midpoint of November 2010 — two sets of believers, two groups with faith in their guys to carry the day.

Baseball (or football, basketball, tiddlywinks) is not transcendent. Its teams play to win and for money. We, the people, pay to see the athletes in action. We believe: we display our faith by attending the games and buying the T-shirts and other accoutrement that indicate our allegiance.

The million or so Giants fans who celebrated their victory in San Francisco were quoted often in the press and on TV as expressing their faith in this odd assemblage of athletes: "We believed in them."

In a similar fashion, the Tea Party people continuously expressed their faith in the message their spokespersons were promulgating. They were strong enough this first time out to push their faith higher. They could be singing, as the civil rights movement sang in the 1960s, "Deep in my heart, I do believe, we shall overcome some day."

No, I don't think that would be their song of choice. Maybe they could get someone to write some new words to that old favorite, "Take Me Out to the Ball Game."

Beauty and Struggle

They are a spectacle combining great personal danger, extraordinary athleticism, and gorgeous performances — performed by innumerable physically attractive human beings.

It's fun to watch the Winter Olympics. Heretofore-unheard-of events parade across the TV screen. Ski cross? Snowboarding? Women's aerials? The skeleton? And more. How can they do that stuff?

The beauty of the dances and the figure skating events exemplify what the human body is capable of doing — lithe and supple, the performers seem to exhibit perfect control over their minds and muscles.

But the dances, the aerials, the figure skating, the ski jumping, and other entertaining contests have scoring systems that make me yearn for ice hockey, where the winner is the team that puts the puck in the goal the most times.

The TV interpreters attempt to fill me in on what counts — whether a body part hits the snow during the landing; how straight her legs are as she twists through the air; how she uses her arms; and on and on. It all flashes by me so quickly, I often can't count the revolutions, twists, and turns accomplished by the athletes.

They are astounding physical beings. My newest physical therapist has worked with a variety of athletes in his career, and he compares these Olympic stars with the ballet professionals he encountered several years ago. He said he was no fan of ballet when he went to work with them and was astonished at what their dances demanded of them — and how hard they had to work at their profession.

I missed the climactic final event, the hockey game between the Canadian and American teams. Reading about it later, I felt that in some way I had deprived myself of participating in their epic struggle. I would have been cheering for the Americans, but it is, after all, Canada's national pastime.

While the players were playing, I was off marveling at the daffodils at Filoli. This was my first trip to this gorgeous parkland, graced with a lovely mansion built between 1915 and 1917.

The place was packed with visitors come to see the spring flower show. Not just daffodils, but hyacinths and tulips as well. Later in the year, the 242 varieties of roses will come into bloom. It will be time to go back.

Back to the daffodils. I plant the bulbs every year and enjoy over 100 blossoms in the front garden and more out back. The flowers are varied in color — yellow, white, white-gold, multiple flowers on a single stem — harbingers of spring.

The heavy rains, while welcome because of the recent drought, have served to beat down some of my blooming beauties. Then, with a sunny day, they become upright again.

In a way, the daffodils' struggle mirrors the athletic careers of some of the Olympic stars. "Beat me down," these winter sport heroes seem to say. "And be ready — I'm coming back."

A stretch of the imagination, but beauty comes in many forms and so does our need to appreciate it and to recognize that struggle is a part of life.

Once, while I was suffering excruciating pain on my left side, my wife drove me to Kaiser's Emergency Hospital in South San Francisco, where I was helped out of our car, loaded on a gurney, X-rayed, and diagnosed with a ruptured bowel. Immediate action was needed to save my life.

Quickly then, a phone call to Redwood City to find a specialist, a painkiller, an ambulance ride, and then the specialist ordered a new X-ray. Re-diagnosed — a kidney stone. One night in the hospital and then home.

Since then, about 1970, it's been mostly minor stuff — a broken bone, tennis elbow, and monitoring of my blood pressure and cholesterol. Much of this had been handled by my long-term physician who is now ill.

In the last two years, there was sciatica and spinal stenosis that have caused pain when I walk or get up after sitting for a long time. So, the advice is to stay active and do the prescribed exercises twice a day.

I'll continue this regimen under my new physician I met today. She, like her predecessor, is an Asian woman with lots of energy.

"Should I take our planned trip in July to Peru?" I asked on first meeting my new doctor.

"Be sure to call the travel nurse to get the correct shots" is one level of advice she gave.

The more important advice was, "Keep on living."

A Spring Sport Experience

It's called March Madness, but it stretches into April. With April, spring becomes more spring-like, and the horse hiders take the field.

Professional basketball enters its playoff season soon, and the puck pushers are closing out their regular season before beginning their championship series. The track types are getting in shape for their first big contest. Tennis is there, and the Masters Golf Tourney is in mid-April. *Jockism* is in bloom throughout the land.

And there is rowing, a tremendous individual and team sport. While there are individual contests, most attention goes to the eight-man-plus-coxswain team battles. It was in this sport that I lost my last opportunity for athletic greatness.

It was a pleasant day — meaning no rain — in early February 1949, that I was recruited for the freshman crew team at Cal. As I came to the last stop in the registration process for my first college semester, two students approached me with an offer I could not refuse.

I was six foot four and about 190 pounds that were a long way from being all muscle. The two crewmembers were not as tall as I but looked very athletic. Cal's team had won the 1948 Olympic title in London, so their pitch involved the winning tradition at Cal and the great opportunity this was for me to be a part of Berkeley history.

So it was that I began a three-day-a-week trip to the oar house to crew around.

There was much to be learned. There had been a group of frosh rowing since September, and they would be the nucleus of the spring team.

The crews — freshmen, JV, and varsity — were head-quartered on the Oakland Estuary across from Alameda. The newcomers were consigned to the barge — a large, heavy, sixteen-oared vessel — where we had to learn how to bevel our wrists on each stroke and use our legs to power our ungainly boat. We sat upon sliding seats. Our stroke would commence when we were hunched over the front end of the slide and then, as we dipped the oar into the water, we moved backward. When we completed the stroke and pulled our oar out of the water, we moved again to the front of the slide.

For a certified klutz like me, it was a bit of a struggle to get this pattern down. And then there was the teamwork. "In and out together" was the chant. The coxswain dictated the speed of the stroking cycle.

When we had achieved at least a low level of proficiency, we made the jump to a shell, the type of boat used in races. Our first shell was a much heavier version of the actual racing shell.

It was about this time, as our group was getting used to the shell, that I learned there was someone with a klutziness potential that dwarfed my own. One of my fellow late arrivals had been a classmate of mine in junior high school, but I hadn't seen him in over three years until we met at practice.

At our second or third try in a shell, he managed — and I don't know how — to stick his foot through the bottom of the shell. Several of the oarsmen had the task of holding the boat against the pier, which prevented us from sinking and possibly injuring my friend.

So there we were, two graduates of San Francisco's Aptos Junior High School, trying to gain fame and glory through our strength and endurance. Not quite supermen, but on our way.

It all ended that June. I don't know what happened to my friend Tony. I know he didn't go back to the oar house, and I never saw him again. I was invited back for fall workouts, but

I took a road less traveled and became a sports reporter for the *Daily Californian* and eventually the sports editor.

The lesson to be learned? I don't know. Maybe it's trying beats not trying.

AFTERWORD

I hope you have enjoyed reading these essays. In French, the word *essay* means "to try; attempt." These essays are my attempts to respond in a personal way to events, ideas, and trends in my life and the life of our country.

As a certified geezer, my experiences and views have the credibility, wisdom, and probably some bias that "supposedly" come with my age. "Supposedly" is a big word! In the end what I have created is a collection of my reactions to where I perceive we Americans are at the end of the first decade of the twenty-first century.

I make no claim to be chief geezer or spokesperson for the rapidly growing class of *geezerdom* that we inhabit. My hope is that these essays generate a response, a spark, thoughts, feelings in you — be you a geezer or a pre-geezer — and that you share your responses with others, especially in cross-generational discussions.